MEDIA 2.0 (18)

MEDIA 2.0 (18)

An Insider's Guide to Today's Digital Media World & Where It's Going

PETER CSATHY
Chairman, CREATV Media

ISBN: 1978375697
ISBN 13: 9781978375697

TABLE OF CONTENTS

ACKNOWLEDGEMENTS ·ix
PREFACE ·xi
INTRODUCTION · xvii

**PART I – SETTING THE STAGE – CREATORS,
CONTENT & STORYTELLING** · 1
Chapter 1 Welcome to Content's New Golden Age · · · · · · · · · · · · · · 3
Chapter 2 The New Media 2.0 Creators & Celebrities · · · · · · · · · · 9
Chapter 3 Media 2.0's New Troubled Waters · · · · · · · · · · · · · · · 13

**PART II – AND SO, HERE WE ARE (THE STATE
OF MEDIA IN 2018)** · 19
PART II, Section 1 – Today's Multi-Platform Video World · · · · · · · 21
Chapter 4 Netflix and Other Premium OTT Players (or Wannabes)
           ("The New Faces of the Content Industry") · · · · · · · · · · · 23
Chapter 5 Disney v. Netflix – What It Means
           (And Is the Threat Real?) · 59
Chapter 6 HBO, ESPN & The Newly Unbundled Stand-Alone
           OTT Video Players (Less Taste, More (Ful)Filling?) · · · · · 65
Chapter 7 Mobile-First, Millennial-Focused Video Companies
           (The Artists Formerly Known as "Mcns") · · · · · · · · · · · · 73

Chapter 8   Traditional Media's Digital-First Reality Check
             (And M&A Mission) · 101
Chapter 9   All Media is Social (or Is It the Other Way Around?) · · 105
Chapter 10   Don't Forget About the Brands! (Or, "And Now a
             Word ... I Mean, Video ... From Our Sponsors") · · · · · 113
Chapter 11   The Mainstreaming of Live Social Streaming · · · · · · · · 117
Chapter 12   Ten Strategies for Today's Media 2.0 Video World · · · · 121
PART II, Section 2 – Today's Digital-First Music World · · · · · · · 131
Chapter 13   The Rise & Dominance of Music Streaming
             (& The Industry's Youtube "Problem") · · · · · · · · · · · · 133
Chapter 14   Music's Streaming Wars (Can Any Pure-Play Win
             Against the Behemoths?) · 139
Chapter 15   A Special Word to Music Artists ("Don't Fear
             the Streaming Reaper") · 151
Chapter 16   Creators – Issues to Consider When Using Music
             in Video & More · 155

**PART II, Section 3 – Our Immersive New Media 2.0 World
of VR, AR & MR** · 159
Chapter 17   VR – The Virtual Gets Very Real · · · · · · · · · · · · · · · 161
Chapter 18   AR – Significantly Augmenting Its Early Success · · · · · 169
Chapter 19   VR, AR & The Great Unknown · · · · · · · · · · · · · · · · 181
PART II, Section 4 – Other Emerging Media 2.0 Platforms · · · · · 185
Chapter 20   A Word About Games & Esports · · · · · · · · · · · · · · · 187
Chapter 21   Offline, Live Experiences (The OFT-Forgotten
             Multi-Platform Plank) · 191
Chapter 22   Social Impact & Media 2.0'S Unprecedented Power to
             Do "Good" (The Stealth Plank, Rising ...) · · · · · · · · · · 197

PART III – MEDIA 2.0 NEWS YOU CAN USE · · · · · · · · · · · · · 201
Chapter 23   Media 2.0's Top 10 Lessons · · · · · · · · · · · · · · · · · · · 203
Chapter 24   Media 2.0 Investment and M&A: Issues to be
             Considered For Both Sides · · · · · · · · · · · · · · · · · · · 213

**PART IV – 2017 YEAR IN REVIEW & WHERE MEDIA 2.0
IS GOING IN 2018 & BEYOND** · 227
Chapter 25   A Look Back at My Predictions for 2017 · · · · · · · · · · · 229
Chapter 26   2017's "Fearless Five" · 237
Chapter 27   My Top 10 Media 2.0 Predictions for 2018 · · · · · · · · · 243

PART V – SO, WHAT DO I DO NOW? · · · · · · · · · · · · · · · · · · · 253
Chapter 28   How to Act Fearlessly in 2018 and Beyond · · · · · · · · · · 255

**EPILOGUE – A PERSONAL NOTE FOR OUR
INCREASINGLY DIGITAL, VIRTUAL AGE** · · · · · · · · · · · · · · · · 257

ACKNOWLEDGEMENTS

For last year's inaugural edition of this book, I essentially flew solo. Not this year. I learned my lesson and smartly enlisted the help of several very smart and dedicated people, including CREATV Media's very own research mavens Ken Aslanis and Joseph Umana. Ken and Joseph uncovered nuggets that otherwise would have remained in the ground, enabling me to significantly refresh and expand this book. I also thank CREATV Media team members Andrea Nunn and Steven Rahman for all of their overall support during the past year. They are both great and extremely talented.

This time, I also more actively sought out the sage thoughts of others, including Greg Akselrud and Jordan Bromley. Both are highly respected media-tech business attorneys with whom I have worked, and each contributes a new chapter that gives more "news you can use" content of the kind that many of you found to be so helpful the first time. Greg, a leading voice in the L.A. media and tech scene, is a Partner in Stubbs, Alderton & Markiles, a top L.A.-based media-tech firm with which CREATV Media partnered during 2017. Greg writes about key issues surrounding strategic investment and M&A, recurring media and technology-related issues that should be of great interest to just about all of you reading this book.

Meanwhile, Jordan is a Partner in the music group of Manatt, Phelps & Phillips and is one of the leading music attorneys in the land. His chapter discusses music licensing for creators who wish to add music to their videos, games, VR and AR experiences – essentially anything. That means his new chapter applies to just about all of you reading this book.

Finally, a general "shout out" to any of you who picked up this book in its first incarnation and deemed it sufficiently worthy to pick it up again this time around. Some of the content may look familiar, but most if it is entirely new. It is significantly expanded, updated and enhanced. Essentially a new book. I took great pains (and drank a lot of coffee) to make it fresh. My hope is that it will be even more useful to you this time as a resource that you turn to over and over again throughout the year – and that, as you do, you breeze through it with the same positivity many of you expressed to me the first time.

Thanks to all. All the feedback. All the support. And all the passion and innovation that gets me jazzed to write this a second time.

PREFACE

Here I am, nearly 30 years into the long and winding road of my career in media, entertainment and technology – a career that I certainly didn't map out. But, precisely because I didn't map it out, I have had a front row seat to a broad swath of technology's ongoing and increasingly relentless transformation of the media and entertainment business. I have been a studio executive immersed in content (Universal Studios, New Line Cinema, Savoy Pictures), a digital media entrepreneur and CEO immersed in the technology that enables and delivers it (Musicmatch, SightSpeed, Sorenson Media), and for the past several years a media and tech advisor, connector, dealmaker and investor.

I took all these disparate and diverse threads from my own personal business "story" and weaved them together to form **CREATV Media**, a media and technology-focused business development, advisory and investment firm. My team and I work with both U.S. and international clients of every shape and size – big media and technology companies, yes, but also major brands and a broad base of privately held companies, entrepreneurs, creators, artists, service providers, and venture capitalists.

All along the way, I have also been a writer, regularly contributing to leading media and tech publications that include *Variety, TechCrunch,* and *Billboard,* and blogging since 2006 and with over 1,700 posts under my belt at *Digital Media Update* (a name that is becoming increasingly anachronistic amidst the reality that all media is digital). I have invested countless hours in trying to make sense of it all, and am fortunate to have direct access to key innovators, entrepreneurs, executives, investors and influencers who make it happen.

And, oh yes, last year I published my first book – the precursor to the one you now hold in your hands and the pages of which you turn "digitally" *(as in, with your fingers, assuming you defy convention and go print)* – which became an Amazon bestseller *(thank you for that!)*. Well, this is round two. I have significantly updated and enhanced it for 2018, of course, adding several new interviews with leading industry executives and updating all key news, metrics, companies, trends, and predictions. I have also significantly expanded it, adding several entirely new chapters and giving significantly more international coverage, not to mention re-organizing the book's overall structure and re-working several chapters to help make better sense of it all. So, even if you read *Media 2.0 (17),* I am confident you will find this 2018 version to be "fresh" and even more helpful and worthy of your time. It is essentially an entirely new book.

In any event, as a result of my writing and speaking, players across the media and tech ecosystem frequently ask me to share my perspectives and give the current lay of the digitally-driven land in which their businesses sit and compete. And, I am told these sessions are extremely useful and impactful.

THAT was the motivation for this book in the first place. It is my attempt to share those insights, those key developments, those leading players, so that you have a much better understanding of the world of tech-infused media and entertainment than you did when you turned the first page.

And to do it in a way that is immediately informative – immediately actionable *(yes, as in, immediate ROI!)* – and hopefully a little entertaining too.

Here's how I lay it out.

Part I sets the stage and underscores that creators, content and storytelling are at the heart of this overall discussion – the foundation for everything within these pages.

In Part II, I discuss the media and entertainment world's *current* state of play in our increasingly virtual and technology-driven multi-platform world – and offer ***a snapshot of what it looked like as 2017 ended and 2018 began*** – so that you have the context you need to take action. Because I can't cover it all, I focus my discussion on the worlds of Internet-driven video (so-called "over-the-top" or "OTT" video), music streaming, virtual reality, augmented reality, mixed reality, games and eSports – without forgetting that live "offline" events and experiences are also fundamental elements of any true multi-platform story. I identify today's leaders and innovators and discuss both how they broke out of the pack, and yet how they too continue to be vulnerable. Remember, no one has it all figured out. They too must continuously act, and their actions and experiments offer clues to where the world of technology-infused content is going.

Part III lays out specific "news you can use" – concrete strategies and actions that flow from the earlier discussions and that you can take to become a hero within your own organization.

In Part IV, I offer my annual predictions for media-tech in 2018, after first looking back at my 2017 predictions with a scorecard that lays out this past year's key headline stories (and how I did in predicting them). I also, once again, christen my **"Fearless Five"** – the five companies that, in my view, made the boldest and most audacious digital media-related moves of 2017.

AT&T topped my inaugural list last year with its $85 billion bid for Time Warner and its launch of its DirecTV Now streaming video service. Who will top 2017's second class? Read on ....

Finally, Part V ties it all together to help you think of what to do next to become an active participant – and change agent – in these technology-transformed media and entertainment times.

Three important things to keep in mind as you read this book.

First, remember that it is intended to be a **snapshot**, the details of which will blur by the day (kind of like a disappearing Snapchat or Instagram Story) due to the accelerating rate of change that is characteristic of these digital times. I take my snapshot here as of the first of November 2017 due to publishing realities, which means that several elements of my discussion may have changed by the time you read this. I recognize that it is a bit anachronistic to write a fixed book about an industry that frequently changes significantly (and sometimes even radically) on a weekly, if not daily, basis. But, many have told me that they needed – but couldn't find – a go-to resource. Something that grounds them. Lays it all out with enough, but not too much, detail. That's my hope here. And, as I indicated last year in my first edition, I plan to update it annually, taking a new snapshot as each year passes, so that it will be a continuing – and increasingly useful – resource for you and your teams. This is year 2, so at least I've made it this far.

Second, let me be clear – I identify companies that **I believe** are leading players or innovators in the world of Internet and technology-driven media based on conversations with industry insiders, influencers and my own analyses. That means that subjectivity permeates these pages. Some of you will agree with my perspectives and certain names and companies I include in (or omit from) this book. But others won't. That's all part of the fun, though. Stirs up some great debates. And, great debates lead to new perspectives. New perspectives lead to new ideas. New ideas lead to innovation. And, innovation leads to transformation. That's ultimately what this book is all about – transformation of the world of media and entertainment at the hands of evolving technology.

Finally, solid, credible sources support every factoid or outside perspective. Sometimes I identify them (like the many industry leaders I interviewed for this book, including Otter Media President Sarah Harden, former CEO Mike Hopkins (and now Chairman of Sony Pictures Television as of year-end), Paramount Futurist Ted Schilowitz, and leading digital media investor Allen DeBevoise). Many times I do not. Not necessarily conventional, I know. But, this is intended to be a relatively informal and entertaining "read," so rest assured they exist. If you have any doubts about any of them, just reach out to me. Challenge me.

So, with those three things out of the way, let's do this – for the second time! Hopefully, bigger, bolder, and better than we did it the first time, so that this book becomes – in the words of my favorite Amazon book review from last year – your *"New Media Bible."*

Audacious, perhaps. But, that's the way you gotta be in our ever-evolving multi-platform world of media and entertainment.

INTRODUCTION

We live in a brave new digital world – where technology drives new transformative ways to connect, communicate, share, sell, entertain, influence and impact. Disruptive new ways to tell stories, find an audience for those stories, and enable that audience to engage with those stories (and with each other).

Just look around you. Everyone you see right now is likely online, looking down, desperately clutching his or her mobile phone – and holding it virtually every waking hour (and increasingly while sleeping to measure night-time success). Why? To "connect" (albeit, virtually), collect, consume and share ever-increasing volumes of content. Some of that content is social. Some educational (even health-related). Some is motivational and inspirational. Others, marketing and commerce. And much of it is entertainment (and increasingly entertaining).

All of that content – those stories – no matter how good, bad, impactful, commercial, or not – are media that now, for the first time, have the opportunity to reach virtually anyone, anytime, anywhere on the planet over the Internet and through that mobile device. Through that extension of the self. Our lifeline in this borderless world. After all, we now live in a world with more mobile devices (7 billion!) than people on our planet. Just think about that reach.

I call this technology-infused content revolution "**Media 2.0**" – and its accelerated pace over just the past few years has been astounding. Media 2.0 impacts all of us. In ways we realize, but many *(most?)* we don't, and won't until we look back years from now. It's up to content creators and the ecosystem that supports them – including business executives, marketers, distributors, investors, technology enablers, students – to seize that opportunity and make content that is impactful, effective, engaging. And, if creators successfully accomplish those goals, then here's the most exciting part – that creator will not be alone in getting the message out. Now, invisible armies of messengers will do that for them. I like what I see, hear or read, and I tell two friends … and so on … and so on. I – on the receiving end – become the re-broadcaster. Check this out – a whopping 92% of mobile video viewers share those videos with others.

Here's just one example of that power. We share a clever little video en masse – which then goes viral – and transform a tiny upstart e-commerce company into quasi-lifestyle media company Dollar Shave Club that Unilever acquired in 2016 for $1 billion. Or, as I wrote in last year's book, together, we transformed a lonely kid in Sweden into social media superstar PewDiePie with 50 million subscribers around the planet and a payday of well over $15 million in 2016. Ahh, what a difference a year makes in Media 2.0 land. In 2017, PewDiePie transformed himself right out of our collective psyches with his anti-Semitic and racist rants, lost it all, and re-entered the ranks of the lonely kids. Yes, the gods giveth, and the gods taketh away! (a highly valuable lesson to all of our kids in our "what happens online, stays online" Media 2.0 world).

Of course, as with any tectonic *("tech-tonic"?)* shift, potential seismic downsides exist. After all, technology – which enabled creation of the mass media and entertainment business in the first place – has threatened it ever since. Evolving technology, by its very nature, disrupts the order of things. Established rules of the game. Lucrative business models.

Consider this fun fact – which ain't so fun for the traditional global advertising agencies. Google and Facebook now own essentially 2/3 of the increasingly cannibalizing global digital ad market! And, how about this one? In a late summer 2017 letter to "The Donald's" top trade official at the White House, Internet and technology behemoths Google, Netflix and Amazon boldly anointed themselves *the new faces of the American content industry, winning Emmys and Oscars"* – and that was even before Hulu became the first video streaming service to win a "Best Outstanding Drama" Emmy. If that ain't a Media 2.0 wake-up call, then I don't know what is.

That's why when faced with a changing world of technology, which will always be the case (radio with television, and television with the Betamax, just to name two), fear and loathing understandably permeate the ranks of those in power in "traditional" media and entertainment. The immediate instinct by many is to either ignore that technology or lash out against it.

But, you know what? In all of these cases – including our current Media 2.0 digital revolution – technological advancements and transformation ultimately led to more overall media and entertainment content consumption and overall industry success, not less. Technology expanded the overall pie. Massively. Deloitte Digital reports that American adults set new records for content consumption in 2016 by engaging in 10 hours and 39 minutes of media daily. Just chew on that factoid a bit.

That doesn't mean that there is no pain, of course. There always is in periods of technology-driven disruption, and I am not minimizing that. The king of traditional media himself – Steven Spielberg – struck a sobering note in 2017 at the opening of USC's new School of Cinematic Arts, predicting a massive *"implosion"* and *"paradigm shift"* relating to long-established business models in the overall film industry at the hands of new digitally-driven realities. Perhaps not necessarily what the crowd on hand wanted to hear as they pondered their future media and entertainment careers, but they needed to hear it. The simple truth is that many relevant content-driven players will, in fact, change over time and some even disappear *(Blockbuster anyone?)*.

But, you know what? The overall market and monetization opportunity has always gone in one direction only – up and to the right. New multi-billion dollar content-driven public companies emerge in record time. Take Snap, for example (parent company to Snapchat). Snap is very much a Media 2.0 company – and went public in 2017 with a multi-billion dollar valuation after only five years of life. Yes, Snap's value diminished significantly post-IPO, but then again, the same thing happened to Facebook after its IPO, and look at Facebook now. So, take heart Snap investors, there is room for optimism in a Media 2.0 world where fortunes can change literally overnight.

In any event, new business models ultimately emerge and settle in based on new rules of the game established by those industry players who take action. Who are **_fearless!_** That's the opportunity here, even if the jury is still out about whether record digitally fueled content consumption can translate into record content monetization.

So, I am optimistic that our current digital revolution ultimately will do the same for the world of media and entertainment. After all, although the forces behind it can be unsettling, frequently daunting and even outright scary, they also offer never-before-possible game-changing opportunities. More stories to tell, and more ways to tell them. More audiences to find, and more ways to reach them. More opportunities to monetize.

And, here's the exciting part. If creators and those supporting them do their jobs right, Media 2.0 also gives consumers a windfall. More high quality content that speaks uniquely to them as individuals. More compelling stories – from more voices – offering more perspectives. More stories consumers will re-tell to their own networks. Everyone wins, or at least has a shot of winning, so long as they take action.

And that's Media 2.0's punch line – its fundamental lesson and universal truth. ***You can't harness Media 2.0's power and potential to thrive (let alone survive) if you aren't in the game in the first place.*** Passivity holds no role in our Media 2.0 world. It is a time for action, not reaction.

Why did the television business settle on the twenty-two minute sitcom format with eight minutes of commercials to round out the half hour? Why did the movie business settle on specific fixed release windows? Why does terrestrial radio pay no licensing royalties to music labels and artists when online radio does? Certainly these realities weren't preordained by some higher power. And, they aren't just historical anomalies. Those who took action at the time defined those realities. Boldly. And these and other rules of the game still hold today – decades later – and have defined the allocation of hundreds of billions of dollars to players in the overall media and entertainment space over the years. Shouldn't those rules be re-imagined now amidst new multi-platform realities? And, if so, is it better to be the re-imaginer or re-imaginee? *(Yes, that's a rhetorical question).*

20th Century Fox Film CEO Stacey Snider – a pillar of "traditional" media – likes the first of those two choices. She represents those fearless enough to understand that the traditional order of things must evolve. That's why she calls for closing fixed motion picture release windows via so-called "PVOD" (paid video on demand) to capitalize on newly-possible unmet consumer home viewing demand that leaves potentially massive sums of money on the table. She predicts that pent-up demand – and the ability to satisfy it – will finally make PVOD a reality in 2018. So, why fight that inevitability? Why not satisfy all relevant players in the overall equation by giving everyone – including theater owners – a piece of the action for enabling an entirely new and potentially extremely lucrative revenue stream? Movie theater subscription services offered by the likes of highly-regarded Turkish-born Sinemia – which entered the U.S. market in 2017 – may be another new way to expand the pie for all. Significantly.

So, act upon the need to "act." Start some fires internally. Hire the best teams you can, and strip out layers of bureaucracy to empower them. *Don't just say that, do it!* Invest significantly in understanding Media 2.0. Experiment – even if you don't have "it" figured out – like a convincing traditional business model. Take solace in the fact that no one does. Things move too fast and the old rules likely simply do not apply. Rapidly iterate. Create, but fail fast, destroying what doesn't work and starting anew. Be tenacious. Relentless. Otherwise, the competition – indeed your entire business – may pass you by.

I call this mind and action set "*fearless media.*"

So, let's get fearless!

Part I

● ● ●

SETTING THE STAGE – CREATORS, CONTENT & STORYTELLING

Last year, I jumped right into the leading Media 2.0 companies and services that are transforming the overall tech-infused media and entertainment landscape. That now follows in Part II.

This year's model that you hold in your hands – or, more likely, swipe on your Kindles – starts with the fundamental foundation for everything else discussed in this book. That is, the content itself. After all, it's the creators, their stories, their content that create the Media 2.0 opportunity in the first place. And, never have great storytellers and their stories been in such high demand.

Content is king. Always has been. Always will be. Especially now.

It's a good time to be king in our always-evolving multi-platform Media 2.0 world.

Read on ….

Chapter 1

● ● ●

WELCOME TO CONTENT'S NEW GOLDEN AGE

Amidst the maelstrom of technology shattering decades-old media-centric business models – a reality that continues to frighten many in its wake – often lost is the fact that we are now in the midst of a new golden age of content. Yes, it's true. There has been too much doom and gloom, and not enough of the content creators' boom. We will look back at this era decades from now as being a period of creative boom, not bust. And you already know why – the Internet, mobile, social media trifecta is already ubiquitous in much of the world. Creators have new power to reach just about anyone, anywhere around the globe, at any time with their stories. And we, the audience, help them expand that audience.

But, it's not just about new distribution models and engagement that are enabled by these new technologies. New forms of content – new artistic freedom – are now possible. Gone are the days of creativity being locked into serial 22-minute segments dictated by traditional broadcast time slots and ad spends. Digital media has shattered those constraints, unleashing a torrent of unprecedented creativity. Content creators have more ways than ever before to express themselves. Those ways are truly unlimited, because mass storytelling has been democratized. All of us can have a public voice – and most of us now do. We can tell the stories we want to tell. Some may be "traditional" in form, but others most certainly are not.

And, here's the deal. An audience exists for *all* of it – both the traditional and the new. These forms don't necessarily compete with one another. The mere fact that our mobile phones are with us and connected 24/7 means that each of us has more (not less) of an opportunity to consume. And, consume we do – voraciously. All of us like to experience a good story, and we enthusiastically embrace new ways of telling them. In my view, we are nowhere near so-called "Peak TV" – a term used by many in the media world to connote commoditization and the high level mark for premium scripted series – precisely because traditional notions of scripted series *(traditional notions, period!)* have been disrupted, upended.

And that's a good thing!

In fact, we are in a new "Golden Age of Content." Great for creators – more demand for their services, more opportunities to tell new stories, and more ways to tell them. And, great for consumers – who now have more content choices than ever before and can (and will) judge for themselves whether specific content is worthy of their time. Have you seen so-called "TV" lately? In 2017, the scripted series count reached 500, essentially doubling the total count just six years earlier. Netflix alone developed about 10% of those, and plans to raise its scripted series total to 80 in 2018. That's a lot of content experimentation. Contrary to those warning of Peak TV, Media 2.0 story telling is significantly *less* formulaic and *higher* quality than it was in the past.

Gone (or, at least certainly fleeting) are traditional cookie-cutter sitcoms and dramas. Now we live in an entertainment world where the most celebrated scripted series *Game of Thrones* kills off lead characters with reckless abandon and where *Fargo* (one of this Minnesota boy's favorites) serves us with a brand new hot-dish storyline and cast each season.

We sample this, binge that. As new media juggernaut Netflix's Kevin Spacey so eloquently underscored in a notorious speech from a couple years back, binge viewing – and other new Media 2.0 phenomena – work precisely because *some* consumers want it that way. Not all, but some. Netflix simply offered a new type of content package, a new mode of consumption. But, it's not binge viewing versus traditional scheduled viewing. It's not a zero sum game of either/or. It's simply a new game with different experiences.

And it's not just a volume game either, where those like Netflix that produce the most, win. HBO scored 29 Emmys to Netflix's 20 in 2017. And FX, led by President John Landgraf (a central voice raising Peak TV red flags), won significantly more Emmys than Netflix in 2016 (18 compared to 9) even though its original scripted series count paled. Yes, there will be more clutter and "noise" out there. But, we consumers can and will decide what *we* like. What speaks to us. What is worthy of our time. We can be discerning.

Not surprisingly, Netflix agrees. At *Vanity Fair*'s 2017 New Establishment Summit, never-afraid-to-be-controversial (in other words, fearless) Chief Content Officer Ted Sarandos proclaimed that *"the notion of Peak TV is a completely backwards idea, which is that somehow you can have too much of things. That's like having too many choices at the buffet. You're only going to eat the things you like."*

And, if we do like something, we will share it with our friends – frequently with real conviction and passion – in digitally-fueled ways never before possible via our social networks, blogs, and Twitter which, despite its continuing business challenges, still delivers reach and impact (just ask larger-than-life TV star of *The Apprentice* ... er ... "Mr. President"?). That's how Media 2.0 works. That's the beauty of it all. Media democracy in action.

But, creators, your audience shouldn't be expected to do all the content discovery heavy lifting by itself. It's your responsibility too. Challenge yourselves to lead the charge, get your voices heard, your stories seen. Media 2.0 gives you innovative new marketing tools that you should *(scratch that, must)* try. Learn by doing. Social media's impact goes without saying, with new innovations popping up all the time. Unearth them. Study them. Use them. Data can be a friend here and should not be simply dismissed as being anathema to the creative process. Data holds the power to better target audiences with content that speaks to them with a voice they want to hear.

Take that quest for data and multiply it with the promise of artificial intelligence ("AI") and machine learning. AI holds potential tantalizing power to deliver the ultimate audience feedback loop where stories and marketing messages are precision-tuned in real-time, thereby making them more relevant and meaningful for distributors, advertisers and we, the people, who need to deal with far less clutter and noise as a result.

And don't even get me started on the promise of blockchain technology for creators and content owners because, as I write this, I wouldn't know where to begin *(you can bet there will be much more on this topic in next year's book)*. Think of blockchain as a tamper-proof, transparent digital ledger. Despite what you may think – if you are even aware of this technology – it serves as the foundation for much more than bitcoin and financial transactions (although so-called cryptocurrency will certainly open up new media and entertainment monetization possibilities). Suffice it to say that blockchain, conceptually at least, holds the disruptive power to create a direct creator-to-consumer path, thereby squeezing out middlemen distribution services *(think about that YouTube and Netflix)*. Blockchain technology also holds the tantalizing power and potential to wipe out piracy.

So, perhaps overall audience size for each program will be smaller amidst the increasing volume and choice of stories. But, perhaps these audiences will be more global. More engaged. More meaningful. And, accordingly, more monetizable. Media and entertainment companies, these possibilities are real.

Embrace this new Golden Age!

Yes, many traditional voices may fade away amidst challenging new Media 2.0 economics (a harsh reality, I know). *Variety* reports that typical production budgets for high-end cable and streaming dramas now range between $5 million-$7 million per hour. Which players can sustain those new Media 2.0 economic realities? FX's Landgraf strikes a sobering tone. In response to questions from *Variety* about Netflix, Amazon and the new Media 2.0 world order's impact on traditional cable networks, he laments that *"Platforms will damage or destroy a lot of brands but not every brand."*

But, the not-necessarily satisfying Media 2.0 response to Landgraf's point is that several more innovative, quality, fearless voices will rise up to be heard – voices that may have more impact on each of us as individuals. Voices that are served up to us as individuals within services that evolve with us, are personalized to us.

This is Media 2.0's great promise and potential.

It is also Media 2.0's simple reality.

Chapter 2

• • •

THE NEW MEDIA 2.0 CREATORS & CELEBRITIES

So, Media 2.0 has fundamentally transformed the media and entertainment business, and this central theme will increasingly hit home as you read on. It has also transformed the very notion of storytelling and "celebrity" in this day and age – not only what it means to be a star, but also who that star is in the first place.

Digital native millennials "think different." They just do. Ubiquitous high-speed Internet, social media and mobile have wired their brains differently, with different sensibilities that are, in many ways, refreshing. Traditional notions of celebrity are evolving fast as a result.

Yes, millennials still obsess over Kanye and Kim, but many of the celebrities that matter most are digital-first creators. In a 2017 study commissioned by Defy Media, significantly more millennials between ages 13-24 said that they would trust a brand or buy a product recommended by these new social influencers more than those recommended by a traditional movie or television star (63% compared to 48%). And 2016 Q Scores showed that fan engagement with these new celebs is stronger than with traditional celebrities like Oprah *(okay, maybe not Oprah because she is, after all, Oprah – but you get the point)*. Why? Because these new celebs are relatable. Approachable. They are just regular kids who somehow amassed frenzied grass-roots followings using new Media 2.0 platforms like YouTube, Facebook, Snapchat, Instagram or now-defunct Vine which grew long fast, but was cut short in 2016 (in yet another Media 2.0 cautionary tale of how fast things change even for once-leading players). These new Media 2.0 celebs rose to the top by starting at the bottom. They weren't anointed from the top down. And, that makes them and their voices authentic to their fans.

Authenticity is the key word here.

If you have any doubt about the power of new digital native celebrities, then simply attend VidCon – Media 2.0's Mecca that takes place each summer in Anaheim. VidCon represents Media 2.0's gathering of the tribe. I urge each of you reading this book to attend, see and most importantly just "feel" the energy that is unleashed when the virtual online world collides with the real offline world – when throngs of 10-20 year old kids scream and swarm every time they see their favorite creator or Media 2.0 star in their very own form of Beatle-mania.

One famous VidCon tale from a couple years back underscores how much the media world has changed for this new millennial audience. Legendary media mogul Jeffrey Katzenberg took the stage for a fireside chat following a panel of digital-first execs and celebs. As he did, a substantial number of the young people in the audience left the room. To be clear, this is no slam on Katzenberg. He absolutely overflows rooms in the traditional media world.

But, that's the point. Nothing is "traditional" anymore. Doesn't mean that motion pictures, television, movie theaters and live events have no role in this brave new world. It just means that those so-called traditional media platforms are now part of the overall multi-platform media ecosystem and world in which we live. For media execs. For marketing execs. For creators. For celebrities. For consumers. For all of us.

Fortunately, Katzenberg is one long-time traditional Media 1.0 player who fully "gets" this – got it early – and got in early. That's why his DreamWorks Animation was amongst the first major traditional media companies to place a big Media 2.0 M&A bet and acquire digital-first media company AwesomenessTV. As we will see later in Chapter 7, it paid off big time and he did just fine.

How will he fare with his second Media 2.0 mega-move, WndrCo, which he launched in 2017 and interestingly hearkens back to Media 1.0 in many ways?

Well, read on. I'll tell you in Chapter 7.

Chapter 3

● ● ●

MEDIA 2.0'S NEW TROUBLED WATERS

Media 2.0's power to unleash creative expression is an extremely positive force. Great for creators. Great for consumers. And great for those in the middle that enable and empower that connection.

Now for some downsides.

I. RAMPANT PIRACY & HACKING

We live in a world where many share the belief that content is free – which means that we live in a world of fast-growing piracy of movies, television, music and all media. Yet, most of us don't know that. In fact, most believe that earlier rampant piracy has been significantly curtailed by new legitimate services and business models like subscription streaming. But, it just ain't so.

Cisco forecasts that file sharing in North America will grow a massive 51% in the five years ending in 2019, and analyst firm NetNames, in a study commissioned by NBCUniversal, concludes that virtually all of that P2P file sharing violates copyright. On the music side, Bain & Company is reported to have concluded that recorded music sales would be 17 times higher in a piracy-free world. And, on the video side, an epidemic of massive hacks continued to scar the motion picture and television landscape in 2017, stripping *(nay, outright stealing!)* hundreds of million dollars (or more?) out of the hands of creators and content owners.

In 2017, hackers notoriously targeted *Game of Thrones* over and over again with their troubling and highly illegal backhanded "compliment." Hackers essentially held HBO hostage in the summer and demanded millions in ransom payments, underscoring that hackers increasingly target Hollywood to steal from creators. Amidst that grand theft, 2017's Mayweather-McGregor epic boxing match wasn't the only big fight of the year. Showtime, owner of the relevant pay-per-view rights, battled with 239 illegal live-streamed rebroadcasts that reached 2.93 million viewers worldwide according to content-security firm Irdeto. What did that cost everyone in and around the ring? Sadly, we have come to the point that media and entertainment companies now consider hacking and related remediation efforts to be ongoing costs of doing business.

Piracy robs creators, plain and simple. When I spoke with Alex Ebert, lead singer of one of my favorite Indie bands Edward Sharpe and the Magnetic Zeros and a tech innovator himself, he emphasized piracy's impact on creators. *"Piracy degrades the craft,"* he lamented. The act of creation is an artist's work – his or her livelihood. Circumventing payment to access, consume and enjoy the fruits of that work (music, movies, television) is like asking someone to build you a house (or even a doll house) and then refusing to pay for it. No one can defend that.

The result? The creative community has been hit where it hurts most – their livelihoods, threatening many from the very act of creation that the most egregious pirates proclaim they purportedly foster through their illegal actions. Ebert passionately punctuates this point, underscoring piracy's potential to create what he calls a generation of *"hobbyist musicians"* unable to focus their lives on the arts, and our enjoyment of it. *"To master anything, you must be able to devote your whole life to it,"* he explains to me – something that is increasingly difficult for many creators whose monetization has been chipped and stripped away.

In Ebert's eyes, that means a generation of lost art – songs, shows, movies, videos that we will never hear or see.

II. MEDIA 2.0 COUNTER-MEASURES

So, what can and should we do about this?

First, we must accept the reality that Media 2.0 disrupts traditional media and entertainment business models and requires a new very different kind of creativity – creativity to define new ways to reach an audience, engage with them, and more effectively monetize them (while respecting and delighting them at the same time). That means business model and marketing experimentation, as well as content experimentation and direct audience engagement.

Second, we all know, at least intellectually, that piracy is wrong. We need to educate new generations and those prone to piracy about its chilling effect on the creative process and the works we will never see as a result. Artists and creators – who increasingly touch their fans via social media and other Media 2.0 modes of engagement – are in the best position to do this. Their fans will listen to them.

Finally, we need to embrace technology. Blockchain technology *(mentioned earlier in Chapter 1)* is most fascinating here. Blockchain technology holds the potential to fundamentally transform the content industry through the use of cryptographic "hashes" of original media files. According to Deloitte, *"a blockchain would ensure that copyright theft and illegal file-sharing become all but impossible."* Strong words, to be sure, in a world where virtually nothing seems impenetrable. The media and entertainment industry – and the artists in it – should significantly up their focus, experiments, and investments in these break-through tools. Indie British artist Imogen Heap is an innovator here. And, Ujo is a leading company in this blockchain mix.

Other newly available piracy-combatting tools – including those that enable the industry to target the most egregious pirates with precision – also should be part of an overall plan. Check out 2017-launched LA-based HAAWK, which offers that kind of state-of-the-art technology.

But, even more important, focus on developing better user experiences. Use new marketing tools. New social tools. New engagement tools. Develop a new language for the new millennial mindset and new Media 2.0 realities. In other words, take positive, constructive action as your first line of defense.

III. NEW DISTURBING CONTENT THREATS

Sometimes it's not the hacking or piracy. Sometimes it's the content itself.

In that regard, two notable and downright terrifying Media 2.0-related unintended consequences reared their ugly heads in 2017. Live streaming entered the mainstream, and live streaming carries very live and very real risks. As a result, tragic acts (including suicides) and crimes (including torture and murder) streamed live to the world on Facebook Live. And, despite all good intentions *(and I absolutely believe Facebook has them)*, it is impossible to police the massive numbers of live streams involved. The best policing comes from us, the audience, who are exposed to these horrors. It is up to all of us to first immediately report such tragedies and crimes and, second, immediately turn them off. Stop rubbernecking for god's sake!

The rise of Neo-Nazism, white supremacists and hate in general – the ugly flames of which our purported "leaders" fanned *(let's be real about that)* – represented a second tragic societal development in 2017. Social media behemoths and content distributors across the board faced this new threat, and many took whatever action they could. Spotify, in one notable example, removed music from a number of self-declared "white power" bands.

Make no mistake. This was no censorship. Non-governmental media and tech companies thankfully have unfettered right to take such actions in the name of overall social good and necessary corporate responsibility – two massively worthy goals. And, while, yes, the First Amendment protects so-called "hate speech," there is no legal protection of any kind when it crosses the line into incitement of violence *(I know, because I represented notorious rap pioneers N.W.A. in just such a First Amendment case when I started my career as a media and entertainment lawyer).*

So, it wasn't all wine and roses in Media 2.0 content land in 2017.

But, let's get back to the positive power and potential of our brave new Media 2.0 world. Let's now turn the page to begin our discussion of to-day's Media 2.0 multi-platform market leaders and innovators.

Part II

• • •

AND SO, HERE WE ARE
(THE STATE OF MEDIA IN 2018)

Part II, Section 1

• • •

TODAY'S MULTI-PLATFORM VIDEO WORLD

Having now set the stage, it's time to dive into 2018's current Media 2.0 state of affairs. Let's first start with video.

Apart from when we are actually together in the real, physical world, video is fast becoming *(already here?)* our primary mode of engagement, precisely because we live in an always-connected and increasingly mobile world – a platform that is optimized for video consumption over traditional lengthy textual narratives. How frequently do you see your kids with their heads down Snapchatting, posting to Instagram, live streaming to anonymous viewers, or simply watching a video, even when their friend is right there next to them on the same couch? And we see it with our engagement with content that we expect to be accessible whenever and wherever we want it in our instant gratification world. That's why Cisco forecasts that video streaming will account for 78% of all mobile traffic by 2021.

Section 1 gives an overview of our wonderful new Media 2.0 world of video.

Chapter 4

●　●　●

NETFLIX AND OTHER PREMIUM OTT PLAYERS (OR WANNABES) ("THE NEW FACES OF THE CONTENT INDUSTRY")

nternet-delivered premium video services are the new normal. These are the disruptors – the so-called "over-the-top" ("OTT") services that generally distribute movie and television content across existing network infrastructure. OTTs are not alone of course – traditional live broadcast TV, pay TV and on-demand download and rental services continue to be major players. But, given their increasing take-over of our viewing lives, leading OTT video players (including Netflix, Amazon and Google/YouTube) now audaciously anoint themselves as being the king-makers. In their own words – as expressed in a notorious summer 2017 letter to the White House – *"we are the new faces of the American content industry."* Provocative, for sure. And very true. Also an implicit knock on the overall traditional media and entertainment industry.

OTT players come in three primary flavors and continue to grow share. Significantly. These include "all-you-can-eat" paid subscription video on demand services ("SVOD"), "all-you-can-eat" advertising-driven video on demand services ("AVOD"), and *virtual* multichannel video programming distributors ("MVPD") that generally offer stripped down live pay TV-like packages called "skinny bundles" over the

Internet (in contrast, actual, non-virtual traditional cable and satellite MVPDs deliver content across their own network infrastructure).

Just a couple years ago, most media and entertainment execs scoffed at the notion of "cord-cutting" – consumers ditching pricy pay TV packages for skinny bundles that give them more of the targeted programming they want for a lot less money. Well, even the most ardent doubters don't doubt that anymore. How could they when leading industry trade publication *Variety* screamed *"Cord-Cutting Explodes"* in a September 2017 headline for a story that reported that 22.2 million U.S. adults would leave the traditional pay TV fold by year's end (up 33% from the 16.7 million who ditched their cable and satellite packages in 2016). Or, when Verizon's CFO Matt Ellis told analysts that *"the traditional TV bundle is not long-term sustainable,"* as he reported the news that Verizon's Fios pay TV subscriber losses deepened in Q3 2017. Even traditional players like Turner's CEO Kevin Reilly openly sounded the alarms. Reilly, a top content creator for traditional pay TV, pointed out the obvious for those who looked – that ratings for all but one of the top 20 returning shows on cable collapsed downward, many by double digits.

But, we are now well beyond cord-cutting. Now the industry is beginning to understand that we have raised an entire generation of "cord-nevers" – those refusing to enter the traditional pay TV world in the first place. Most are millennials (so-called "digital natives") who can't even comprehend a world with no broadband Internet and smart phone-driven premium video. That same *Variety* story mentioned above reported that the number of these cord-nevers would rise 5.8% to 34.4 million in 2017. And, get this – cord-nevers will equal cord-cutters in number by 2021, for a combined traditional pay TV-snubbing audience of 81 million U.S. adults.

And, just in case these realities needed to be hammered home any further, Morgan Stanley analysts now value Netflix's Media 2.0 content assets at a whopping $11 billion – more than the content assets of traditionalists

Time Warner ($10 billion) and the combined assets of Viacom ($4.9 billion), Discovery Communications ($2.4 billion), AMC Networks ($1.5 billion) and Scripps Networks Interactive ($1.1 billion). Sobering, yes. But motivating, hopefully, too.

A week doesn't seem to go by without another major new premium SVOD, AVOD or virtual MVPD player entering the game. Disney made the biggest splash in 2017 when it announced in August its own pair of upcoming "Netflix-Killers" *(much more on that later)*. Many compete head-on with Netflix, as Disney is expected to do when it launches. So, even mighty Netflix feels the heat from increasingly intense competition – a level of intensity that was turned up to a spine-tingling, Spinal Tap-ian "11" this past year. (Maybe that's why Netflix – in a major 2017 head-scratching, yet highly effective, marketing campaign – self-deprecatingly pronounced to the world that *"Netflix Is a Joke,"* perhaps signaling that it too understands its vulnerabilities).

A growing number of other kinds of premium OTT video players focus on specific content segments for underserved markets. Examples include AMC Network's "Shudder" for horror-focused programming and "Acorn TV" for British comedies and drama, Turner's "FilmStruck" for classic and indie films, and U.K.-based Channel 4's "Walter Presents" for the best independent television programming from around the world. Still others focus on specific geographic territories rather than trying to blanket the world. Examples here include emerging market-focused iflix (backed by Sky and Liberty Global) and HOOQ (the Southeast Asia-focused SVOD joint venture of international telco Singtel, Sony Pictures Entertainment and Warner Bros.).

This is the backdrop to the frenetically paced, increasingly crowded and competitive premium OTT video world. Here are some of its key players, including their key strengths, weaknesses and recent strategic moves to enhance their positions.

I. THE PURE-PLAYS

NETFLIX – THE INVINCIBLE ONE (OR IS IT?)

Netflix, of course, dominates the premium SVOD market in the U.S. and increasingly overseas in 190 territories. We all subscribe to Netflix (nearly 116 million worldwide as of Q4 2017, up from 86 million one year earlier). In fact, as of early 2017, more U.S. television households use Netflix than DVRs. Pretty astounding, when you think about it. And, for the first time in Q2 2017, the number of Netflix's international streaming subscribers surpassed U.S. subscribers.

We almost instinctively pay a monthly fee ranging from $8 to $12 for higher quality streaming across multiple screens (at least we did – Netflix announced across-the-board global $1 price hikes in Q4 2017). For this, we get unlimited ad-free on demand viewing that covers all programming bases – essentially all genres, everything for everybody – and with an increasing array of high-quality, expensively-produced, exclusively-available original programming *(I call this content category "Originals" as a shorthand throughout this book).* And, unlimited streaming, we do. Collectively, worldwide, we watched more than 125 million hours of movies and television daily on Netflix in 2017. Originals have become Netflix's calling card, continuously winning many of the industry's most prestigious awards (the SVOD giant won 20 Emmy Awards in 2017, second only to HBO's 29).

Due to its sheer size, Netflix has earmarked massive dollars to fund development of its Originals. For 2017, that number ballooned to $6 billion to finance 50+ Originals and license premium content. But, why stop there? Chief Content Officer Ted Sarandos has commit to upping that number to $7-$8 billion in 2018 to develop 80 Originals – with an astounding $17 billion in content commitments already locked and loaded as of Q4 2017 (a number that certainly will continue to escalate, if not accelerate).

Netflix's ultimate goal is to feature a massive video library that is equally split between its own Originals (the costs for which it can control) and the licensed content of others (the costs for which it can't).

Sarandos concedes that Netflix has no choice. The major studios, on which Netflix has historically depended for the majority of its movies and television, increasingly have Netflix in their sights. As a result, they have either significantly raised their licensing rates, pulled back on their licensing, or announced that they will withhold valuable programming completely *(that would be you, Disney)*. In Sarandos's words, *"The more successful we get, the more anxious I get about the willingness of networks to license their stuff to us. That's why original content is critical."* Originals. Plain and simple. That is Netflix's fundamental long-term strategy.

Netflix owns a treasure trove of data about what we watch and how we watch it – and uses that data to inform its content decisions. How much? No one except for Netflix really knows, although Nielsen announced in October 2017 that it can now measure and report Netflix and other SVOD viewing in what it called an industry *"game changer."* Netflix, in turn, dismissed Nielsen's initial reporting as being *"not even close"* to reality and has no plans to release its own data, because why would it? Those traditional metrics hold little relevance to Netflix and its subscription model. Only subscriber numbers, customer acquisition, churn (customer retention), revenues and profits matter. Even Netflix's A-list talent, like the Kevin Spacey's of the world, aren't clamoring for that data, because they too are happy developing their passion projects and getting paid handsomely to do it. It's kind of *"Don't ask, don't tell"* – Netflix edition.

Interestingly, as of early 2016, only about 10% of total Netflix viewing streamed on mobile devices. And, downright shockingly, it is reported that the overall total number of hours streamed by Netflix's U.S. subscribers on mobile devices did not change year-over-year from June 2016 to June 2017, despite Netflix's significant subscriber growth over that time. No surprise then that up to now, Netflix has focused only minimally on mobile-first and mobile-friendly programming that is typically more "bite sized" in length. So, mobile presents a significant opportunity, especially as Netflix expands internationally into emerging markets where mobile is essentially the only screen.

At the same time, mobile – and Netflix's lack of focus on it – presents a significant risk, given Media 2.0's ever-increasing mobile viewing realities. Undaunted, CFO David Wells doubled-down on Netflix's mobile-light strategy in 2017, indicating that mobile at some point will become *"more important, but right now it's about the large screen."*

Here's another major risk to Netflix. Unlike many newly aggressive competitors like Hulu, YouTube TV and DirecTV Now *(all discussed below)*, Netflix has no plans – at least no publicly-revealed plans – to offer a virtual MVPD experience that offers live television channels. That's significant. Very. After all, despite Netflix's seeming omnipotence, Hub Entertainment Research reports that half of Americans still see live TV as being their go-to platform for viewing, whereas only one in five of us apparently go to Netflix first when we need our TV fix.

Netflix's fundamental Achilles heel, however, is its one-dimensional business model. Netflix monetizes only its content. That's very different than mega-competitors Amazon, YouTube TV, Apple, AT&T/ DirecTV Now and others discussed below, all of which can use content purely as marketing due to their fundamentally different multi-faceted business models. So, Netflix's long-term viability as an independent is dependent on both (1) extracting more from its existing customers via price hikes (like it announced in Q4 2017), and (2) expanding – and retaining – its customer base amidst an increasingly-crowded playing field where others hold more pricing freedom and consumer switching costs (i.e., the costs of terminating an existing service) are essentially zero. And, that means "feeding the beast" – our voracious demand and continuous expectation for new compelling premium A-list-driven Originals.

And, as we have already seen, that beast is expensive to feed. That's why Netflix's losses continue to mount and are expected to reach $2.5 billion in 2017 after losing $1.7 billion in 2016. Even more, CEO Reed Hastings conceded to Wall Street that Netflix expects *"to be free cash-flow negative for many years,"* as the company announced another $1.6 billion in debt offerings in Q4 2017 to add to its existing $4.9 billion in long-term debt. Ouch! And, the costs for Originals will only rise significantly over time. They already have amidst hyper-competition in the overall premium video space, in which HBO invests more than $15 million *per episode* for *Game of Thrones*.

Wait. There's more. Netflix doesn't own the rights to many of its most popular Originals. It licenses them. That goes for *Orange Is the New Black*, *House of Cards*, *Iron Fist*, and *The Crown* (which reportedly cost Netflix $10 million per episode). That means that Netflix can't really control those costs. Second, the ever-expanding playing field of OTT video competitors aggressively fight for access to a limited supply of A-list marquee talent that they hope will attract new customers to their service (and keep them there). That means Netflix can't control those costs either, which already have skyrocketed.

Meanwhile, that A-list talent will smile all the way to the bank as they get pulled in multiple directions. In the words of Jeff Wachtel, chief content officer for NBCUniversal Cable Entertainment, *"Actors and writers and directors who used to compete for jobs are now having studios compete over them."*

Good time to be an artist or creator, indeed!

HULU

Hulu officially launched in 2008, backed by NBCUniversal and News Corp. (now 21st Century Fox). Disney joined the party in 2009 and Time Warner joined in 2016, buying a 10% share that valued the company at $5.83 billion. That means AT&T will be a proud part owner of Hulu once it finalizes its $85 billion acquisition. Hulu offers three pay tiers of service: (i) $7.99 per month for on demand streaming with ads; (ii) $11.99 per month for a commercial-free on demand experience; and (iii) "Hulu With Live TV," which gives 50+ channels of live and on-demand television programming (including ESPN) plus the full Hulu premium streaming VOD library for about $40 per month. The full monty of live, on demand and library streaming is Hulu's major differentiator from Netflix, as it tries to move up from its third place position amongst U.S. SVODs (RBC Capital Markets reported late 2017 that Hulu accounts for 18% of the overall U.S. SVOD market, compared to Netflix's 61% and Amazon Prime Video's 41% *(Amazon is discussed below)*. (For those of you math wiz's out there, these numbers total more than 100% because many of us subscribe to more than one SVOD service).

Prior to becoming Chairman of Sony Pictures Television as 2017 ended, former CEO Mike Hopkins told me that Hulu hopes that its new live channels will extend average daily viewing time to *"5 to 6 hours per day,"* significantly longer than typical daily SVOD viewing. That means more customer reliance on Hulu in their daily lives and a deeper overall relationship. And, in Hopkins' words, *"when you have a deep relationship with a consumer, you will find additional ways to monetize that relationship by offering more value."* He cites commerce as being one such possibility. Live is just Hulu's boldest move yet to be a real, credible alternative to Netflix.

Hulu also stepped it up big time a couple years back when it shelled out massive dollars to license the rights to exclusively stream iconic television shows like *Seinfeld* and *South Park* – $180 million and $192 million, respectively. And, Hulu also is accelerating the pace of its own Originals to keep up with the Jones's *(I mean, Netflix of course)*. To that end, Hulu committed $2.5 billion to Originals and overall programming for the U.S. in 2017. Not quite global Netflix-ian numbers, but certainly approaching them. And, with its 10 Emmy wins in 2017, including the Emmy for "Outstanding Drama Series" (a first for any streaming service), Hulu's message to the world is *"Game on!"*

Hulu's greatest strength against Netflix and others – apart from Hulu's new live programming – is its media DNA. Hulu's media roots mean that it holds an advantageous position over others to license – and showcase to consumers – the biggest, and most current, movie and television titles. Let's face it, membership has its privileges.

But, Hulu's media-backed strength is also one of its greatest weaknesses. Joint ventures amongst media companies are notoriously challenging. It is a bit like herding cats *(I know, because I've been there)*. Another weakness – or opportunity, depending on how you look at it – Hulu is available only in the U.S *(Hulu Japan is a separate entity operated by Nippon TV)*. International expansion still seems to be on the back burner. Most challenging, just like Netflix, Hulu is saddled by its one-dimensional business model that monetizes only its content. Just like Netflix, the company must find new ways to expand, monetize and reach profitability.

Hopkins told me that Hulu's formula to succeed is to expand its content pool even more aggressively and offer the best overall customer experience, especially in the areas of content recommendations and personalization. That means that my Hulu experience may look and feel very different than yours. And, that's smart, because a critical consumer "pain point" in our Media 2.0 world is finding the content needle that speaks to you amidst the ever piling up premium content haystack. Hulu put its money where its mouth is in that regard as 2016 ended, buying the Video Genome Project to help fuel its personalization goals.

(As a side note, and speaking of the increasing need to help consumers find ways to sift through that growing haystack of content, check this out. OTTs cannot (and should not) live on recommendation technology alone. Human curation most certainly will play an *(increasingly?)* important role in our customer experiences, which means that Media 1.0 "best practices" shouldn't be entirely discarded. Perhaps some can be adapted to new realities. Case in point, the good old-fashioned movie poster. Leading marketing agencies like Mob Scene in LA see a growing (not declining) need for poster art which, on a smaller thumb-nail scale, increasingly serves as quick visceral clues and cues to drive us to click this title over that one as we scroll through the endless sea of content available to us on all of our various screens.)

II. THE BEHEMOTHS

Netflix and Hulu are the major U.S.-based pure-plays that monetize one thing only – the content itself. Each of these mega-players below, on the other hand, use premium OTT video as marketing vehicles to drive their multi-pronged business models. In that way, they are fundamentally different animals.

AMAZON PRIME VIDEO

Behemoth shopping mall-in-the-sky Amazon launched Amazon Prime Video a few years back and has become a shocking contender, second only to Netflix. Amazon Prime Video lacks the deep motion picture and television catalog of pure-plays Netflix and Hulu, but it too funds development of its own exclusive Originals that draw customers in and have been surprisingly successful (Academy Award-winning *Manchester By the Sea* and Emmy Award-winning *Transparent* being just two examples).

Amazon really stepped up its all-out assault on Netflix in 2017 by investing $4.5 billion in its Originals and overall programming, doubling its expenditures for 2016 in the process. As two examples, Amazon drove a reported $250 million deal for *The Grand Tour*, its blockbuster car show from the team of *Top Gear* – and also recovered Twitter's fumble of NFL *Thursday Night Football* live streaming rights for a reported $50 million. Amazon Prime Video undoubtedly will continue to up its content ante in 2018 like all others.

Just like everyone subscribes to Netflix, everyone shops at Amazon. And, if you're an Amazon Prime subscriber *(because why wouldn't you be ... FREE SHIPPING!)*, then you're already an Amazon Prime Video subscriber, although you may not even know it. That's right. The good folks from Seattle toss in this perk for "free" to Primers – and they do it in over 200 countries *(take that, Netflix which counts a mere 190!)*. But, make no mistake – Amazon does not toss us this video bone altruistically. Oh, no no no. There is most definitely a method to its madness. A tantalizing one.

Amazon Prime Video is a fundamentally different SVOD animal than both Netflix and Hulu in two critical respects. First, you don't pay more for it, so it is difficult to really define how many "subscribers" it has (although *Variety* reports 54 million Prime subscribers in the U.S. alone as of October 2017). Second, unlike Netflix and Hulu, Amazon doesn't need to make money directly from Amazon Prime Video itself. You heard me right. Just like Apple used music via iTunes to lure us into Apple stores for years to buy iPhones, iPads, and Macbooks, Amazon primarily uses Amazon Prime Video to lure us into becoming Prime customers who "shop 'til we drop."

And that fundamental difference gives Amazon a massive advantage over – and significantly more business freedom than – pure-play SVOD services Netflix and Hulu. That freedom includes significant freedom to undercut pricing, as Amazon already is doing in the streaming music world with its Amazon Music Unlimited service *(discussed later in Chapter 14)*. Former Hulu CEO Mike Hopkins previously acknowledged Amazon's advantage, telling me *"it's not something you don't worry about."* But, Hopkins believes that Amazon's strength is undercut by its secondary focus on content. *"[Hulu] will compete better because it's our core product."*

Meanwhile Netflix's Ted Sarandos dismisses the Amazon threat almost entirely. *"I frankly don't understand their strategy,"* said Sarandos in a 2017 *Variety* interview, citing what he deems to be Amazon's unfathomable decisions to release some of its Originals in theaters first, which, in his view, *"perpetuat[es] a model that feels more and more disconnected with the population."* *(You will see in Chapter 21 that I beg to differ, and feel Amazon's actions reflect a brilliant truly multi-platform strategy.)* But, Amazon revels in its counter-programming to Netflix in terms of its release strategy for Originals. Amazon, in fact, now operates its own significant self-distribution theatrical motion picture business and executes its own theatrical marketing campaigns.

In any event, Amazon also holds tantalizing data about us, including all of our shopping habits. It knows what we browse and buy and, therefore, arguably is in a better position to give us better-customized content recommendations. And, because we are already programmed to have our credit cards ready and waiting when we enter Amazon's mall, we may be more open to paying for additional content and related commerce in all of its other non-SVOD forms as well.

That's the tantalizing prospect of video-driven e-commerce, and no one has more of those prospects than Amazon. You can bet this mega-player will make it drop-dead easy to buy NFL merchandise as we watch our favorite teams battle on Thursday nights. How can we resist? Alexa's helpful, soothing voice will make it so easy that we won't need to take our hands out of our popcorn bowls. She likely will even offer flash incentives to get us to buy more – all from the comfort of our couches. How helpful is she?

Amazon Prime Video is intriguing. Very. Amazon is simply, well, just everywhere (including everywhere Netflix doesn't want it to be). To that point, research firm Parrot Analytics reported in 2017 that Amazon was gaining ground on Netflix in Europe, with average demand for Netflix programming dropping 32% year-over-year from early 2016 to early 2017. At the same time, and with a significantly smaller content library, demand for Amazon programming reportedly rocketed 57%. That narrowed Netflix's year-earlier 235% lead over Amazon Prime Video to just 45%. Parrot further reported that Amazon Prime Video even out-performed Netflix in Germany just a few months after launching there.

So, real data backs up the reality that no one – not even mighty Netflix – is a lock. Amazon is knocking. And it has a mighty powerful fist.

Stop. Watch. Listen to Amazon in 2018. It is an incredibly powerful Media 2.0 force.

GOOGLE/YOUTUBE TV

YouTube – still the giant amongst giants in the world of Media 2.0 video – took a Hulu-like path in 2017 to be your premium paid video service provider of choice and take a bite out of Netflix. YouTube launched its own virtual MVPD service appropriately called "YouTube TV" that features both premium on demand and live TV programming. YouTube TV gives you about 50 channels (including, yes, ESPN again) for $35 per month, plus primarily youth-focused Originals via access to its "YouTube Red" service. Unlike Hulu and the other virtual MVPDs discussed in this chapter, YouTube TV keeps it simple, offering only one paid tier of service. No "good, better, best" options here. While YouTube hasn't released any subscriber numbers yet, Bloomberg reported that YouTube TV and new Hulu Live had together signed up only 160,000 paying subs as of July 2017.

Yes, YouTube still also operates its $9.99 monthly YouTube Red subscription service. But, Red-driven Originals star YouTube's top Media 2.0 talent – not traditional marquee Hollywood talent – so it's not really an "apples to Apples" comparison (so to speak). "Red" itself apparently isn't exactly setting the world on fire, and is undoubtedly operating in the *(forgive me)* red as a stand-alone service. It reportedly hosted only 1.5 million paying subscribers as of summer 2016, with 1 million more signed up on a trial basis at the time. After all, it's always tough to get consumers to pay for something that they've used for free for years, even if that "something" is now a very different thing. *(You will see in Chapter 14 that Pandora faces similar challenges on the music streaming side of the house).*

At the end of the day, however, YouTube's definition of "success" with its premium OTT video ambitions can be very different than Netflix's or Hulu's. Does it really matter whether YouTube's services are stand-alone successful? Remember, Google/YouTube is a lot like Apple and Amazon when it comes to content. Sure it's nice to have users pay for it. But that's all gravy. The main course is its underlying, very different core business model. For Google, it's all about serving ads. Keep 'em coming, and you'll do just fine.

YouTube is still the dominant overall OTT video player as you look across the entire spectrum of Media 2.0 video content. But, it is now more challenged than ever before due to the fast-growing media ambitions of another Goliath. Facebook.

FACEBOOK

If 2016 represented Facebook's "coming out" for its media ambitions, 2017 brought it all home and made it 100% clear that this behemoth was all-in against all comers in the world of premium TV-esque video programming. Facebook launched its much anticipated "Watch" service in August 2017 with its own "special sauce" – its always-engaged rabid daily audience of 1.32 billion who inevitably will find, view, follow and comment on those videos. In CEO Mark Zuckerberg's words, *"Watching a show doesn't have to be passive. You'll be able to chat and connect with people during an episode, and join groups with people who like the same shows afterwards to build community.*" And, Facebook makes it drop dead easy to fritter your day away on all platforms, including Apple TV.

"Watch" went out the gates with hundreds of shows, including Originals that Facebook commissioned to seed its catalog. Facebook reportedly committed $1 billion for its initial premium content efforts and absorbed up to $3 million per episode for splash-worthy tent-pole shows. Watch also features programming from Major League Baseball, A&E Networks, National Geographic, Conde Nast, Tastemade, and Whistle Sports, among others. What's the common denominator? According to Dan Rose, Facebook's VP of Partnerships, *"One, they're shows you want to engage in with your friends and family, or co-workers ... around the water cooler. Two, they're shows you want to engage in with other fans, like the way people do with sports."* While Facebook places no time restrictions on Watch programming, generally they will be relatively short-form (10 minutes or so) and all will be recurring/episodic. And, just like much of our own Facebook content, expect most Watch programming to be cute and cuddly and not particularly edgy *(featuring lots of animals, because god knows we love to share our favorite animal videos!).*

Apart from its foundational Originals, Facebook says it doesn't (and will not) pay its founding content partners for the privilege of streaming to their audience of billions. Rather, it shares its ad revenues with the typical industry "55% goes to you" deal. Ultimately, Facebook's long-term plan is to open up its most prized possession, its massive base, to all creators in the community who salivate to reach them and bring the quality goods. Facebook plans to offer thousands of channels.

Facebook now prioritizes video content, because the video ads that flow from that content are significantly more lucrative than traditional text and banner ads (although Facebook's margins on those videos, as Zuckerberg points out, *"almost certainly"* will be lower if it ultimately chooses to invest significantly in its own Originals). In any event, Facebook's video-centric strategy, which up to the launch of Watch focused on pumping content through its Newsfeed, seems to be working.

Like Amazon, Facebook's other secret weapon is its reams of data about each of us who obsessively engage with it over and over again each day. Facebook certainly collects more information about us than just about any other service (except for Amazon), because we eagerly hand it over to them. And, data is power. In the immortal words of Tony Montana – twisted a bit to fit this context – *"You gotta get the data first. Then, when you get the data, you get the power. Then when you get the power, you get the viewers!"*

Amen, Tony. Amen.

2017 was a very good year for Facebook.

APPLE

What about Apple? Well, as 2016 ended, this Goliath's owned and operated premium OTT video dreams appeared to be squelched. Media and entertainment execs felt enough is enough with Apple, still reeling from iTunes' take-over of the music industry well over one decade ago. Well, that changed in 2017, as Apple began investing big time into developing Originals of its own to the (i)Tune of $1 billion. And, of course, Apple will feature Originals like *Carpool Karaoke* exclusively on Apple TV and our ubiquitous iPhones, where it can also give its Originals top billing.

Apple TV, of course, already is a major distribution platform in its own right that offers on-demand downloads and rentals, although its 21.3 million monthly connected users as of July 2017 pale to market-leading Roku which boasts 38.9 million monthly users (AppleTV has a surprisingly low #4 connected-TV market share). Speaking of Roku, this fearless Indie hopes to extend its lead over giants with its massive late 2017 IPO-driven cash infusion, as well as with (you guessed it) its own new premium AVOD service that it bowed in October 2017.

Ultimately, Apple TV, which now features its own Originals in addition to those from other leading OTT video services like Netflix and Hulu, hopes to be your one-stop-shop and guide to all that OTT choice out there – in effect, your Media 2.0 "TV Guide."

So, don't expect Apple's previous relative passivity to last in the current premium OTT video battle royale. Make no mistake, Apple *does* want to offer its own premium SVOD service, and will undoubtedly offer both on demand streaming and live skinny bundles when it does. Apple is both hyper-competitive and a control freak. It's not in its DNA to see others win in a game in which it wants to play. We saw how this played out on the music side. Apple first resisted music streaming services *(remember when Steve Jobs completely rejected them?)*, then waited too long when reality set in, and then failed when it finally launched its own Apple-branded music streaming service. So, what did it do? It bought its way into the music streaming game in 2014 with $3 billion via Beats and is now a top music player again.

That M&A strategy may play out here too on the video side. If Apple can't succeed in getting entirely what it wants on its own as it increasingly battles the other behemoths – which has largely been the case up to this point – why not buy its way in with a player that already has what it needs?

Hmmmm, who could that be? No Dana Carvey, not Satan.

Netflix anyone? Apple certainly has the cash. Audacious, yes, but that certainly wouldn't surprise me, especially now that Disney pronounced in Fleetwood Mac-ian fashion that it will "Go It's Own Way" and compete head-on with Netflix.

Either way, Apple will be relentless when it enters the ring, bundling its SVOD service in all of its Apple TVs and iPhones. Unlike competing services, no separate install or sign-in will be needed. That's some massive automatic and instantaneous distribution. Its second secret Applesauce is user experience. Like Hulu, Apple believes that it can best help consumers make sense of all that content, a problem all of us increasingly face as we are deluged by waves of new high quality premium programming. And, Apple has a proven track record to do that right *(iTunes ring a bell?)*. After all, it holds the tremendous advantage of being able to perfect its user experiences in a closed system that seamlessly melds Apple's services with its products.

DISNEY

Ahh, yes. And then there's Disney. As mentioned earlier, Disney boldly announced in August 2017 that it too will throw its mouse ears into the already-crowded SVOD market and, at the same time, hold back some of its most valuable programming from Netflix (no matter how much Netflix is willing to pay for it). Disney hasn't launched its new SVOD services yet, so we don't know exactly what they will look like. And, even for a behemoth like Disney, widespread adoption in a sea of Netflix, Amazon and other giants certainly will be no lay-up. So, whether Disney's twin SVOD services become the happiest places on earth remains to be seen. Even so, this mega-development – which qualifies as being one of the most audacious (yet, inevitable) Media 2.0 moves of 2017 – is so big that it deserves its own chapter.

Read on. You will find it next in Chapter 5.

SONY CRACKLE AND PLAYSTATION VUE

Sony too is out there in the premium OTT video fray with two very different services. "Crackle" is Sony's Netflix-like SVOD service, while

"PlayStation Vue" is its virtual MVPD that offers live skinny bundles. For now at least, Sony keeps those two OTT services separate.

Crackle's "special sauce" is that it is an AVOD service only – completely free. But, it is a distant player next to Netflix, Hulu and Amazon and its overall consumer awareness pales.

PlayStation VUE, on the other hand, used 2016 to open its doors to the world (not just to Sony gamers) via Roku and mobile apps – and significantly extended that reach to the usual suspects like Apple TV in 2017. VUE offers live programming packages ranging in price from $39.99 monthly for 45 channels (including ESPN) to $74.99 monthly with significantly more, including HBO and Showtime. VUE too is a distant player, with Frost & Sullivan reporting only 400,000 paid subscribers in 2017.

To expand its reach, Sony inked a deal in 2017 to sell VUE through small cable operators that perhaps feel a bit marginalized by the more well established OTT video players. A quaint gesture, to be sure, but likely not enough to make a dent.

Time for Sony to boldly step up its Media 2.0 game.

III. BEHEMOTHS OF ANOTHER COLOR - THE ACTUAL MVPDS

But wait, there's more. With traditional pay TV packages under siege, it was only a matter of time before the actual, not virtual, big cable and satellite MVPDs entered the premium OTT video game. After all, each of them holds the secret weapon of built-in distribution via massive customer bases. They are "locks" to be successful, right?

Well, not so fast. First, before we introduce these Netflix "wannabes," time for another Media 2.0 cautionary tale – this time, starring once-almighty Samsung.

Samsung – an undeniable behemoth with a massive customer footprint – launched its own premium OTT services a few years back and came out swinging. It first launched its streaming music service, strangely called "Milk Music" *(even befuddled Samsung execs conceded to me that they didn't know quite what that name meant or why they chose it).* It later doubled down with that enigmatic brand and launched its premium OTT video twin – "Milk Video" – to great fanfare and investment, including top executive talent. But, alas, nothing happened. Both services fizzled. Samsung first dropped Milk Video in 2015, and then pulled the plug on Milk Music one year later in 2016.

Lesson here? Massive distribution alone does not guarantee massive results, or even meaningful results. After all, consumers can already get the services they really want – like Netflix and Spotify – on virtually any platform. So, why would they sign up for yet another new service, especially if it comes from a name like Samsung that doesn't exactly scream content and storytelling? There must be more to make a dent, and that's where the focus needs to be. A library of exclusively offered premium content (Originals) is the most obvious answer, and Samsung didn't have it. One more key lesson from Samsung's experiment gone awry – far too much bureaucracy and too many layers of management. Samsung hired experienced content execs to lead the charge, but failed to empower them. That leads to low morale, and low morale leads to diminished results. Every time.

But, don't feel too bad for the giant traditional MVPDs below if they fail in their bids for OTT video dominance. Yes, their pay TV subscriber numbers and content-generated revenues may continue to shrink *(in fact, they will shrink – there is nothing "may" about it).* But, many of these companies are now more profitable than ever. Yes, it's true. All of that great high quality premium movie and television video content that streams from other OTTs demands fatter, more expensive broadband "pipes." And, we content-hungry consumers absolutely will pay for that without even thinking about it.

Take Comcast, for example. Its revenues rose nearly 8% in 2016 from one year earlier, with broadband penetration being its largest growth factor. Here's another one. Altice USA, owner of Cablevision and Suddenlink (the fourth biggest cable group in the USA), saw its revenues rise 5.8% and operating profits skyrocket 25.3% in Q2 2017. And no end is in sight for these and other purveyors of pipe amidst our never-sated thirst for faster and faster broadband that brings these plumbers significantly better economics via higher margins.

With this background, let's see which of the major actual MVPDs moved into the online-delivered virtual MVPD world in 2017 (or at least announced plans to do so).

AT&T/DIRECTV

AT&T, that's who. Not exactly "trying." More like massively doing. AT&T made 2016's boldest and brashest Media 2.0 mega-move by buying venerable Time Warner and its treasure trove of Warner Bros., HBO and Turner content for $85 billion. AT&T launched its all-out premium OTT video assault on Netflix and the others in November 2016 under its "DirecTV Now" banner after acquiring DirecTV for $50 billion in one of 2015's boldest moves.

DirecTV Now counts about 800,000 subscribers as of Q4 2017, including 300,000 gained in Q3. At the same time, however, DirecTV lost 390,000 – so does that mean that DirecTV Now is cannibalizing? In any event, DirecTV Now features both VOD and a baseline skinny bundle of 60+ channels (including ESPN) for a monthly $35 price point that caused shock and awe when it was first announced, and which placed tremendous pricing pressure on all others when they entered the ring. No mystery, then, that Hulu priced its entry-level Hulu Live bundle at roughly the same number. DirecTV Now also offers higher-end packages with about 80, 100 and 120 channels at a monthly $50, $60 and $70, respectively (and included premium channel HBO for no additional cost during the year as an incentive in advance of its Time Warner closing). So, DirecTV Now's packages aren't too skinny after all. They are, in fact, the fattest in the virtual MVPD industry.

These relatively reasonable "a lot for a little" monthly fees likely mean that AT&T operates its new virtual MVPD as a loss leader to build overall market share and play an Amazon-like long game in a hyper-competitive market. And, in a competitive edge, AT&T wireless subscribers can stream DirecTV Now on their mobile phones without dinging their wireless plans. Net neutrality be damned!

Assuming that AT&T successfully closes its Time Warner deal *(it's still in The Donald's tiny hands, after all, as I write this in early November 2017)*, DirecTV Now will control the premium video trifecta of Warner Bros., HBO and Turner. That's some powerful content ammunition that it can deploy in new and potentially exclusive ways – and also withhold from those with whom it does battle a la Disney's announced plan with Netflix.

For those of you skeptical of AT&T's ambitions and likelihood of premium OTT video success, I'd offer a word of caution. AT&T already is everywhere in many of your lives, and DirecTV itself is a long-time content-focused mega-player largely due to the NFL package. Don't forget that AT&T via Time Warner also will be a part owner in Hulu, which means it will have two horses in the premium OTT race (essentially competing against itself with DirecTV Now and Hulu once that deal closes).

AT&T also is a strategic partner with The Chernin Group in its $600 million-ish Otter Media joint venture. Underscoring that commitment, DirecTV Now features Otter's millennial-focused Fullscreen SVOD service *(which I discuss later below)* as a further differentiator. That's a third horse in the premium OTT race. So, AT&T has placed multiple premium OTT video bets and is a true multi-platform player – an extremely formidable one at that. In fact, when AT&T successfully closes its Time

Warner deal, it will also be an immediate significant player in the tantalizing new worlds of virtual reality and augmented reality that I discuss later in Chapters 17 and 18.

One of the big questions for Media 2.0 in 2018 and beyond is whether AT&T's new "whole" will be greater and more valuable than the sum of all of its massive individual parts. It will be fascinating to watch.

There certainly is no denying that this formerly stodgy company has fundamentally transformed itself in just the past few years and is now absolutely a fearless Media 2.0 leader.

VERIZON

AT&T's arch-nemesis Verizon entered the premium OTT ring big time itself in late 2015 when it launched its mobile-first "Go90" OTT streaming video service that is focused on younger millennials ages 16-24. Why "Go90" (which apparently changed its lower case "g" to a much more aggressive cap "G" this year)? Don't ask. Okay, ask. Turn your smart phone screen 90 degrees to horizontal for video viewing and, voila, you are "going 90." Get it? (*Well, maybe the kids don't, because millennial Snapchat-transformed mindsets are decidedly vertical ... but, I digress.*)

Verizon itself invested massively in content in 2016 when it made one of that year's most audacious moves – its comparatively bargain basement, content-fueled purchase of long-languishing Yahoo! for $4.8 billion (a price tag that dropped to $4.48 billion when the deal closed in 2017, due to the purple Y's unearthed and highly-publicized hacking woes – *but why quibble over a mere $350 million?*). And this was after having acquired AOL just one year earlier for $4.4 billion in another content-driven Media 2.0 mega-move.

Go90 continues to open its pocket book widely to commission premium mobile-friendly Originals from leading digital-first media companies *(which I discuss later in Chapter 7).* Word on the street from the creative community in 2016 was that Verizon seriously overpaid for exclusive rights to their content, spending $200 million and frequently between $1-$4 million per bite-sized show (according to *Business Insider*) in an effort to differentiate its service from the others and fuel Go90 adoption, much like Netflix did when it first launched its Originals strategy. But, Verizon significantly turned down its cash spigot in 2017 after realizing how difficult it is to lure millennials away from their existing "go to" services simply by mega-reach and a mega-dollar-fueled content strategy – hard lessons already learned by Samsung and Yahoo!

Many industry insiders are skeptical of Verizon's ambitions as a result of Go90's early results (or lack thereof) and because the company has been down this content road before. But, Verizon now, for the first time, has powerful new Media 2.0 DNA in the form of executives from AOL and Yahoo!, which they combined this past year into an overall content/media unit called "Oath" (a name which, as one industry insider joked to me, might not be the worst name ever, simply because Tribune Media's truncated "Tronc" still is ... *I thought that was pretty funny).* Both AOL and much-maligned Yahoo! have serious content chops. They just didn't make the most of them on their own. Maybe Verizon can help. It certainly has some proprietary platform technology after acquiring sinking digital-first video innovator Vessel late 2016.

With all these big bets, it's certainly no surprise that Verizon also threw its hat into the AT&T/DirecTV Now-ian ring by year-end 2017, announcing that it too plans to compete more directly with premium content on all platforms and to a mass audience via its own hoped-for "Netflix-Killer" *(or at least maim-er)* – not just to young millennials via Go90. Multi-tentacled Verizon also plays in the OTT video space via two separate mobile-first video joint ventures – "Complex" (with Hearst) and "AwesomenessTV" (with Hearst again, and Comcast).

Verizon throws a lot of spaghetti against the wall to see what sticks. A strategy that I don't condemn at all. Better to take action than stand frozen in time.

COMCAST NBCUNIVERSAL

Speaking of Comcast, Comcast NBCUniversal is also all over the map in this brave new digitally fueled and increasingly cord-nevered video world – and with mixed results so far. Comcast, of course, already is a major OTT player via its joint venture ownership interest in Hulu. And, the conglomerate went much further in 2016 when it placed a continuing string of significant Media 2.0 bets that included buying DreamWorks Animation for $3.8 billion (acquiring kids-focused digital-first media company AwesomenessTV in the process, a company that I discuss at length in Chapter 7). In 2016, NBCUniversal also launched comedy-focused SVOD "Seeso" *(as in, "see" … "so"?)* to complement Comcast's mobile-first, millennial-focused, ad-supported OTT service "Watchable."

But, monetizing digital-first video is hard. The SeeSo experiment apparently "saw so" by 2017, as NBCU announced by August that it would shut it down by year's end. At about the same time, Comcast also announced that it was shuttering its Flixster Video streaming and download service. And, it wasn't done yet. In rapid fire, Comcast also announced that it would eliminate Watchable's funding for Originals and essentially simply keep that service on life support. Kind of a late "boys of summer" 1-2-3 strikeout. But, as I wrote last year, we are still early in the Media 2.0 video game, and I applaud Comcast NBCUniversal for trying, experimenting, *learning.* That's the key part – i.e., learning.

Soon we will see how that learning is going, since Comcast announced in the second half of 2017 that it too would enter the SVOD cage match against Netflix and the other giants, even as it already prominently bundles Netflix on its X1 set-top boxes. Comcast's upcoming SVOD – titled

"Xfinity Instant TV" – will apparently cost only a fraction of the others (about $15 per month). How, you ask, can Comcast justify this dangerously low fee? Well, Comcast Cable's CEO Dave Watson explains that his plans are not to go wide with this mobile-first, millennial-focused SVOD. In his words *"this is going to be very targeted, primarily digital in a nature in how we do it."* Hmmm. Sounds a lot like Verizon's Go90 ….

Beyond these moves, in Q4 2017, NBCUniversal announced a new 50/50 joint venture with Snap to produce mobile-first scripted content. Comcast also laid out its plans late 2016 to become your wireless carrier of choice, using its valuable content and overall presence in your lives as its "special sauce." We didn't hear much more about these audacious plans in 2017. But, if the company does move forward, then you can bet that Comcast will feature premium NBCUniversal content not available anywhere else in the wireless world and efficiently bill you for that privilege.

And, don't underestimate the power of convenience.

DISH/SLING TV

I discussed DirecTV already in the context of AT&T. So, how about DirecTV wannabe DISH? That's an interesting question, because DISH hedged its Media 2.0 bets earlier than most. In 2015, and in a bold move to appeal directly to the accelerating number of cord-cutters and cord-nevers, DISH brashly launched its skinny bundle-laden virtual MVPD service. Notably, Sling TV was the first to offer ESPN a la carte, in a snub to all pay TV services out there that counted ESPN as the glue to hold those supersized bundles together. Sling charges $20 monthly for its basic package of 30 or so channels that now includes ESPN for no additional charge. From there, you have the choice to upgrade to a higher-end package or even individual channels like HBO at its stand-alone $15 per month price.

Sling TV is reported to have reached the 2 million subscriber count as of Q3 2017, which sounds pretty good. But, early returns lead many to believe that DISH essentially cannibalizes itself via Sling TV, since DISH lost 196,000 pay TV subs in Q2 of 2017 alone (a number that includes both satellite subscribers and Sling TV subs). Kind of what AT&T seems to be seeing with DirecTV and DirecTV Now.

But, then again, would you rather cannibalize yourself or passively let the OTT competition cannibalize you? I'll take Door #1 please!

MAJOR CAVEAT – CONSUMERS BEWARE!
All of these virtual MVPD services carry their own programming and technical "hits" and "misses" in these early days. Many lack some of the major broadcast networks like CBS (which means that a stand-alone CBS subscription must be purchased separately), and several miss your favorite cable channels like Comedy Central *(and we all need a little Trevor Noah, don't we?)*. Most also have limited DVR capability and other use restrictions, including the number of permissible concurrent streams – meaning that you may not be able to watch TV in your room while your kids watch in their rooms. And, many are simply just plain glitchy right now. But, make no mistake – these services are knocking down these very real issues rapid fire in real time. So, while 2017 represented the great onslaught of the virtual MVPDs, 2018 will represent their maturation and very real cut-the-cord alternative and choice.

IV. INTERNATIONAL PREMIUM OTT PLAYERS

Those are just the U.S. mega-players in the global premium OTT video game. But, even in today's political climate, let's not be overly nationalistic and focus on domestic players alone. After all, it's a big, borderless world out there. So, yes, while Netflix operates in over 190 countries and

Amazon ups the ante to 200-plus, here's at least a taste of other major international players, many of which have their own designs to win beyond their own borders.

CHINA

Let's first take China – the biggest international prize of them all – where multiple mega-companies vie to be the "Netflix of China."

Netflix itself first tried to do it. On its own. But, then reality set it in, and Netflix held up the white flag of surrender late 2016. Rather than fight the inevitable, it smartly chose to switch strategies and partner – finally cracking the code (at least to a limited extend) in the process. Netflix chose China's popular video platform iQIYI (a subsidiary of Chinese search giant Baidu) as its dance partner in 2017, which made Netflix programming – but, importantly, not the Netflix service itself – available to this new mass market. So, Netflix chose to hit a single, rather than keep swinging for the fences. iQIYI, on the other hand, now holds a particularly strong claim of being the coveted "Netflix of China." After all, it now has the Netflix content to prove it. And, you guessed it, iQIYI plans to build on that claim via an aggressive Originals strategy of its own. But wait, there's even more. As year-end 2017 approached, Baidu announced that it may seek a U.S. IPO for iQIYI in 2018.

Other China behemoths are investing massively to beat back iQIYI and take the pole position. They include the usual suspects – uber-brands Alibaba (through its Youku Tudou side of the house) and Tencent (which in 2017 became the exclusive live streaming partner for the NFL in China). Wanda Cinema Line, the world's largest cinema exhibitor, also entered the SVOD theater this past year via Mtime (China's answer to Fandango and IMDb), in which it made a $350 million investment. And, in an interesting twist, Hong Kong-based Bison Group signed a deal to acquire a majority stake in struggling U.S.-based OTT player and platform Cinedigm to not only conquer China, but also to bring Chinese content to a U.S. audience. You know, the old "what's good for the goose is good for the gander" play *(what's a "gander?" I ask, with my best George Castanza impression).*

(As a separate side note related to that deal, China's government cracked down significantly in financing further foreign media-related investment and M&A in 2017, especially in connection with the Wanda Group's aggressive plans in that regard. Wanda had previously acquired AMC Entertainment and Legendary Entertainment).

In last year's edition of this book, I discussed LeECO, another then-major Chinese player that proudly proclaimed itself as being the "Netflix of China." And, from the outside, life looked good for LeECO in 2016, as it boldly announced that it would introduce its new SVOD service both in China and in the U.S. to compete on Netflix's home turf. The company had even acquired a 50-acre site from Yahoo! in Silicon Valley for $250 million to do it! How audacious and downright cocky is that? But, in yet another Media 2.0 cautionary tale, LeECO crashed and burned less than twelve months later in 2017 in what represents a stunning fall from grace. First, the company scuttled its highly publicized $2 billion acquisition of television-maker Vizio. Then, the floor completely dropped when LeECO essentially cancelled all of its plans for U.S. OTT market domination and laid off hundreds of U.S. workers.

Two lessons here kids. Lesson #1 – effectively launching and monetizing digital-first video services is increasingly hard amidst the growing field of behemoths. To wit, LeECO (and don't forget about enterprise video darling Vimeo, which also dropped its Netflix-ian direct-to-consumer plans in 2017 after announcing them only months earlier in November 2016). And, Lesson #2 – internationalizing your customer base is even harder. Netflix and LeECO are proof positive of that point. So, if you want to be a formidable player in another major territory outside your home turf, the answer is not to go it alone. You must partner – and *"sit down, be humble"* when doing so (in the poetic words of Kendrick Lamar, one of 2017's breakout artists).

OTHER NON-EUROPEAN EMERGING MARKETS

Exhibit A to that partnering point is HOOQ – the joint venture amongst major telco Singtel and competing media giants Sony Pictures Entertainment and Warner Bros. HOOQ launched in 2015 as a mobile-first SVOD service that operates in Southeast Asia and India. In 2017, HOOQ announced significant early success when it crossed the 1,000,000 paid subscriber mark. And then there's Hearst, which led a $133 million round of financing in emerging market focused SVOD iflix *(yes, the company uses no caps – now that's innovation!)*. iflix reported 5 million customers as of May 2017 and operates in nineteen countries and territories in Asia, Southeast Asia, the Middle East, and North Africa. Backed by international media giants Liberty Global and Sky (as well as CAA-affiliated Evolution Media Capital), the service hopes to beat back Netflix with a hyper-focus on hyper-local content, as well as better pricing that it believes is more in line with the realities of those consumer markets. That means $2-$3 per month rather than Netflix's $10 monthly pricing.

iflix's outspoken CEO Mark Britt, in true audacious, contrarian fashion (in other words, entrepreneurial and fearless), confidently proclaims that he and his team *"don't believe the thesis that Netflix is going to achieve a global monopoly."* He points out that iflix launched well ahead of Netflix in *"places nobody else cares about"* and identifies Vietnam, Myanmar, Sri Lanka, Pakistan and Saudi Arabia as specific examples. He also claims to take a country-focused approach rather than viewing broad territories monolithically, which means more localized content and culturally-specific user experiences. Smart. Very smart. And, eversly Disney is helping iflix in its counter-Netflix-ian cause. Specifically, while Disney plans to hold back flagship content from Netflix, it did a George Castanza-like opposite *(yes, there he is again)* and actively helped iflix launch a Disney branded channel that features its biggest franchises, including Marvel and Pixar.

Other hyper-local competitors in Southeast Asia include "Tribe" (an SVOD owned by Malaysian pay TV group Astro) and "Catchplay" (which launched in Taiwan but now also operates in Indonesia and Singapore at a $5 monthly fee). Meanwhile in Korea, and in an interesting twist, three of the country's largest broadcasters partnered to launch a new OTT service called "Kocowa" that is laser-focused on a U.S. audience hungry for Korean dramas and K-pop (you know, the same audience as Warner Bros.'s "Drama Fever" OTT video service).

Not surprisingly, the Japanese market is also crowded. Japanese e-commerce giant Rakuten operates "Viki," a two-tiered AVOD and SVOD service that is available in 195 countries and boasts over 1 billion viewers (and is surprisingly based in San Francisco). And, six of Japan's biggest media companies, together with TBS (an interesting Media 2.0-ish U.S. addition to that list), announced plans this past year to launch their own premium video service called "Premium Platinum Japan." But, their combined $72 million investment in this startup is microscopic compared to investments made by the other behemoths discussed above. And, you gotta go big to have a real chance to win big (or even make a dent).

How about India? Here are some to consider. "Spuul" features premium video content from Bollywood, and others include "BIGFlix," "BoxTV," "YuppTV" and Star TV's "Hotstar." And, in Russia, that tundra-laden country's Google is Yandex, which is now very much focused on video in an effort to confine Netflix to Siberia.

EUROPE

I leave Europe for last, simply because Netflix and Amazon are already major established players there, with Amazon (as discussed previously) reportedly catching up to Netflix and now becoming a real threat. But they certainly aren't alone either. U.K.'s Sky is a major Euro-focused SVOD player with 22.5 million subscribers across the U.K., Ireland, Italy, Germany, Austria and Spain. Its strategy, of course, is to beat back Netflix and Amazon with its own slate of localized Originals, including the popular *Babylon Berlin* in Germany.

Other players – both obvious, and some not so much – plan to join the party. As year-end 2017 approached, German media giant ProSiebenSat.1 announced a 50/50 joint venture with Discovery Communications to launch a new premium OTT video service for the German market. Deutsche Telekom is said to be mulling over its own SVOD to compete in the land of lederhosen. Meanwhile, all of Europe's other major telcos – including France's Orange, Spain's Telefonica, and the U.K.'s BT – announced significantly expanded Originals strategies to more effectively compete in the SVOD market with their own localized content. Even good old-fashioned Turner – yes, Time Warner's Atlanta-based Turner – surprised virtually everyone by outbidding all others to pick up rights to Europe's top UEFA Champions soccer league. Turner apparently plans to launch a new sports-centric SVOD with global, non-U.S., football at its core. Finally, in a nod to my Magyar D.N.A. *("Magyar" is what we Hungarians call ourselves)* – and to underscore the need to be hyper-local in order to succeed against global giants – services like Hungarian-based MoziKlub sprinkle in their own local SVOD content flavor (in this case, paprika). *(By the way, here's my Hungarian lesson for you – "Mozi" means movie ... and "Klub" means, well, think you can figure that one out).*

V. OTHER CHALLENGERS – SMALL, BUT AMBITIOUS

FULLSCREEN

This is an interesting one – with a very different story. Fullscreen sprung out of the world of multichannel networks *(I discuss those later in Chapter 7)*, aggregating a broad base of YouTube content. Things got really interesting when former

News Corp. President Peter Chernin and his company The Chernin Group – which had first tried, but failed to buy Hulu – leveraged their newfound Media 2.0 knowledge and invested in Fullscreen. Chernin later launched his $600-ish million content-focused joint venture, Otter Media, in 2014 with AT&T and handed over Fullscreen to Otter as part of that deal.

Fullscreen changed course in 2016 and launched its own $5.99 monthly SVOD service to compete more directly against other premium OTT video services. It hopes to win by focusing its marketing – and its own slate of premium Originals – on a young mobile-first millennial audience. Many of those Originals come from Rooster Teeth, a leading digital studio Fullscreen acquired earlier in 2014. CEO George Strompolos tells me that Fullscreen Media is *"the only company in the world with an offering that begins with digital-first talent development and expands into original programming, live events, consumer products, OTT video and brand services."* Not sure if others would agree with Strompolos's claim to be uniquely multi-platform, but it is certainly bold and I respect that. Now it's a question of focus amongst oh-so-many choices. But, early returns don't look bad, as the service proudly boasts over 600 million global subscribers as of fall 2017.

Fullscreen's not-so-secret weapon is AT&T which, of course, calls its massive mobile customer base to tune-in to Fullscreen via DirecTV Now. And, as the end of 2017 approached, rumors swirled that AT&T was in talks to acquire Otter. If true, that will represent yet another major Media 2.0 bet by AT&T which continues to make a strong case to top my "Fearless Five" list for a second year.

See if it succeeds in Chapter 26 … *but don't flip ahead!*

FUBOTV
And then there's FuboTV – away from Hollywood and on the Right Coast in New York. Talk about ambitious! FuboTV launched early 2015 as a sports-centric OTT video service primarily focused on kicking global

soccer matches across territorial goal lines to a U.S. audience. But, over time, FuboTV somehow amassed a total of $75 million (including a massive $55 million infusion in 2017) to significantly expand its entertainment faire and compete more directly on the virtual MVPD pitch against the behemoths via its $39.99 monthly service.

Does FuboTV stand a chance against industry Goliaths? CEO David Gandler tells me that his strategy to win in 2018 is to *"solidify ourselves as the leading sports-first virtual MVPD as we take advantage of strong industry tailwinds to grow our customer base and prove ourselves as a viable alternative to cable or satellite. This includes maintaining a bundle that includes the most sports for the least money."* And, David certainly has enlisted giants of his own to block those Goliaths, counting 21st Century Fox, Scripps Networks Interactive, and U.K.'s Sky as strategic investors. Insiders tell me that even DirecTV Now takes FuboTV very seriously.

Now, the fundamental question is how this upstart can grow beyond its 100,000 paid subscriber base (as of September 2017) and become a significant force in the SVOD space.

VI. WHAT DOES THIS ALL MEAN?
The list of Netflix wannabes is long, and we have just scratched the surface. Several other premium OTT video players try to rise above the premium OTT video din, including Walmart's rarely-mentioned AVOD service "Vudu" (which hopes to win with its re-booted "Vudu Movies on Us" service), "Pluto TV" (an AVOD that raised $8 million in financing from Samsung Ventures and others in 2017 to add to its total haul of $52 million to compete with a throwback cable TV-like EPG-ish customer experience), "Fandor" (an indie and international film-focused SVOD), and "Tubi TV," just to name a few.

One thing is absolutely certain. This proliferation of premium OTT video services shows no signs of abating. Others will rise up, several will fail, and bigger fish will eat many of those caught in the middle. 2018 promises to be a pivotal shake out year in the giant global OTT video market.

So many choices. So little time to watch and pay for them all.

Perhaps former Hulu CEO Mike Hopkins said it best to me with words even more on point this year. *"We're in an absolute knife fight."*

Chapter 5

● ● ●

DISNEY V. NETFLIX – WHAT IT MEANS
(AND IS THE THREAT REAL?)

As teased in Chapter 4, Disney rocked the premium OTT video world in 2017 when it officially – but inevitably – announced its plans to compete head-to-head against Netflix and the other OTT video giants with separate forthcoming Disney and ESPN SVOD services. At the same time, Disney announced that it would no longer license much of its prized content to Netflix. With this 1-2 gut punch, Disney looked straight into Netflix's eyes and pronounced, *"Game On!"*

So, how worried should Netflix and its investors be about the Disney threat and what it represents? In a word, *"Very."*

Here are three reasons why.

(1) Disney is supremely motivated to win. In the past year, Disney had likely wanted to buy – not fight – Netflix to become an instant global SVOD juggernaut. But Netflix apparently had too high of an opinion of itself in the eyes of Disney, at least. And, Disney doesn't like to lose. So, now the gloves are off.

But, more fundamentally, Disney had no choice but to prioritize digital OTT platforms by either buying or competing with Netflix, given the cut-the-cord bleeding of traditional cable and satellite television packages that historically have been Disney's cash cow. ESPN's downward slide in traditional pay TV packages has been well publicized, and the Disney Channel is right there with it. SVOD is Disney's newly-minted plan to make up for that lost ground, and you can bet that CEO Bob Iger will ignite all of his multiple businesses, platforms and channels to promote Disney's new SVOD cause celebre to consumers. Scary indeed.

A bit daunting for Disney too, by the way, precisely because ESPN is widely seen as being the glue that holds traditional pay TV packages together. ESPN is the home for sports, of course, and sports remain one of the last bastions of premium content that consumers feel they need to experience live, rather than on demand. That's why the major pay TV players pay Disney handsomely for that privilege. Extremely handsomely. To a certain meaningful extent, those lofty traditional ESPN economics prop up an entire professional sports ecosystem, including the skyrocketing professional athlete salaries that go with it. And some pundits believe that Media 2.0's unbundling forces will cause those overall industry economics to come crumbling down. So, Disney's SVOD moves, at least to a certain extent, bite the hands that feed by competing directly against its traditional pay TV sugar daddies.

(2) Disney knows that "content is king" like never before amidst this extremely heated SVOD competition, and now plans to use its content might as a weapon to win. Amidst the massive entertainment SVOD global land grab and overall shift to OTT video viewing, exclusive content is the great differentiator. That's why each massive player is trying to capture our hearts and minds (and most importantly, our eyes) with high-priced, premium quality exclusive Originals. Well, guess what, Disney already owns the rights to the most valuable brand, franchises, content and characters in the world. Due to massively astute strategic moves over the past decade plus, ESPN and Disney princesses now share the stage with the Marvel, *Star Wars* and Pixar holy trinity. So, why give industry-leading Netflix the keys to its content castle when Disney can deliver that magic kingdom directly to consumers itself?

Exactly! And Disney isn't. Not anymore. And, make no mistake, that hurts Netflix. Disney-esque kids-focused programming is increasingly strategic to Netflix, since about half of Netflix's subscribers regularly watch kids-focused programming that is frequently animated and uniquely "evergreen" (which means kid-friendly content cost-effectively travels well internationally and never gets old). That's precisely why Netflix immediately countered Disney's gut punch by buying Millarworld, the comic book creators of characters and stories that include *Kick-Ass, Kingsman* and *Old Man Logan.* Those characters are increasingly strategically significant to Netflix now that Disney is gone and its primary focus is international expansion.

Netflix went even further just days later in the supposed dog-days of summer 2017. It stole television creator Shonda Rhimes of *Grey's Anatomy* and *Empire* fame away from Disney/ABC with promises of riches and creative freedom that ABC's traditional media system simply couldn't match. In rapid fire, it also pilfered Robert Kirkman, creator of *The Walking Dead,* away from traditional pay TV player AMC. Two major retaliatory shots across the traditional media bow. Some industry insiders called those Media 2.0 moves not only a blow to Disney, but also to broadcast and cable TV in general.

(3) Disney is just the latest in a long and growing list of far better re-sourced industry behemoths hell-bent on taking Netflix down. That list now includes AT&T's DirecTV Now, Amazon Prime Video, YouTube TV, and Apple – and soon, as we saw earlier, will include upcoming services from Verizon and Comcast. None of these giants will be "Netflix Killers" alone, of course. But, together, this colossal cabal may result in "death by 1,000 cuts" to Netflix (or at least heavy bleeding). Netflix is too big to fail, of course. But, that doesn't mean it can survive long-term on its own. Disney, after all, has a market cap of about $150 billion compared to Netflix's relatively paltry $85 billion as of November 2017. So, Disney – like all the other behemoths – certainly has deeper coffers with which to compete.

Even more significantly, as we see saw in Chapter 4, Disney and the others bask in the glow of a holistic, multi-faceted business model. In Disney's case, it can monetize multiple divisions with multiple product lines and revenue streams (movies, television, theme parks, merchandising, licensing), all on a global scale. Netflix can't. As discussed earlier, its business model is one-dimensional. Netflix's very existence is justified by content subscriptions alone.

Disney's forthcoming SVOD services, on the other hand, just need to play their parts in Disney's overall smooth-running, multi-platform machine. That gives Disney and other mega-competitors like it tremendous freedom that Netflix doesn't have, especially as budgets for Originals continue to skyrocket amidst this hyper-competition. Remember, Netflix spent a whopping $6 billion in 2017 alone on its programming, plans to spend $7-$8 billion more in 2018, plans to add $1.6 billion more in debt on top of its existing $4.9 billion to keep the hits keep coming, and holds long-term content commitments of $17 billion. How long can it keep that up? Disney's call to arms certainly doesn't help Netflix's cause.

Naysayers no doubt will challenge the notion that Netflix, with its global brand and massive head start, faces any real existential crisis from Mickey and his fellow cast of giant OTT characters. After all, all of us reading this undoubtedly count ourselves as being part of the Netflix faithful. Would any of us ever really leave?

Well, chew on this. Each of these three meta-forces discussed above is a massive new threat, the likes of which Netflix has never seen before. First, the onslaught by Disney and the burgeoning list of other major players – all of which can afford to play the long game – now offer real choice to consumers for the first time. Take Amazon for example. As I mentioned earlier, Amazon Prime Video is reported to be gaining ground on Netflix in Europe and out-performing Netflix in Germany only a few months after it launched.

So perhaps in increasingly critical international markets where the Netflix brand is not so deeply entrenched, neither is viewer uptick or loyalty in the face of compelling alternatives. Even in the U.S., consumers face no real switching costs in an OTT world. If they lose interest in Netflix Originals or simply prefer those of Amazon or others, all they need to do is cancel their monthly subscriptions. Yes, many will pay for more than one. But, Netflix's U.S. market penetration already exceeds 50%, and its long-term bet on continuous international expansion faces major headwinds related to significantly higher overseas customer acquisition costs. Not much room for error here in a market that gets ever closer to saturation.

That leads to the second disruptive factor of ever-escalating Herculean budgets for Originals in order to both acquire and retain customers. Amazon, with its more ironclad checkbook, spent $4.5 billion on programming this year, closing in on Netflix's $6 billion in that regard. Ultimately, Netflix foes like Amazon can afford to out-spend the reigning champ – or undercut its pricing – if they choose to do so. How can Netflix keep up?

Finally, Disney's internationally beloved franchises, characters, and overall brand are marketing goldmines that can be used to attract new users – but are now apparently out of Netflix's reach forever. It's not too much of a stretch to assume that Time Warner's movies and television shows will follow suit when AT&T closes that $85 billion mega-deal. Other major media companies have already significantly upped their licensing fees to Netflix or pulled back their content significantly.

Together, these amount to a perfect storm that may stunt Netflx's growth and depress its shares. Maybe not overnight, or even in 2018. But, ultimately, Netflix will not be able to go it alone. Whereas Disney can.

Now for Disney and its OTT ambitions, the pivotal question becomes whether it hires the right talent with the right digital-first DNA and gives them the freedom and flexibility they need to pull it off. So, which leadership team will steer Disney's new multi-platform Media 2.0 ship after Captain Bob Iger leaves the deck in July 2019 (a date that Disney's board keeps pushing back)? And, how intriguing would it have been if Disney had, instead, bought Netflix and installed Media 2.0 kingpin Reed Hastings as Iger's successor?

But, that's not reality.

Netflix against the world – that's reality.

Chapter 6

●　　●　　●

HBO, ESPN & THE NEWLY UNBUNDLED STAND-ALONE OTT VIDEO PLAYERS (LESS TASTE, MORE (FUL)FILLING?)

Media 2.0's great unbundling! That's what I call the new world of once pay TV bundle-only channels that have now freed up either to go it alone or be part of stripped down skinny bundles. Whereas Netflix, Amazon Prime Video, Hulu and the others discussed in Chapter 4 offer an endless stream of content across multiple "channels," stand-alone pay OTT services *are* the channel – frequently focused on a specific genre. You can now access them without being forced to pay for other channels or content you don't want.

Sounds so simple. But it took so long to get here. Now that it has, the number of these newly emancipated OTT services seems to expand almost daily. Here are some key market leaders, each with very different D.N.A.

HBO
Pay TV darling HBO – renown for premium high-quality storytelling – really started this "great unbundling" in a big way in 2015 when it boldly stripped itself out of pay TV bundles to offer itself as a stand-alone SVOD

service at a price-tag of $15 per month. HBO's move represented a major digital-first shot across the traditional media bow – the first domino to fall in a lengthy line of other individual premium pay TV channels that followed. Just months before, many media and entertainment executives predicted that such a move by a major pay TV player wouldn't happen for years. After all, the major cable and satellite providers pay HBO handsomely for carriage. So, why would HBO bite the hand that feeds?

Because HBO saw Media 2.0's writing on the wall, that's why. As already discussed, the accelerating number of cord-cutters and cord-nevers hit home as the industry realized what many consumers already had – why pay for the full content cow when you can buy the milk for free *(well, not free, but certainly for a fraction of the cost)*? HBO risked losing an entire generation of digital natives who simply wouldn't consider buying what many perceived to be overly filling, bloated pay TV packages. HBO wanted to reach them – and is reported to have reached 3.5 million subscribers as of mid-2017 (which still represents only about 3% of HBO's 131 million worldwide subscribers, including 34 million in the U.S.). Hence, the big, bold bet that threatened HBO's relationships with its big cable and satellite partners who shelled out big bucks to carry it and made it the brand we all know today.

HBO held the cards in this poker game. As upsetting and unsettling as HBO's game-changing play was to the major traditional MVPDs, they knew that consumers would bolt to the OTT streaming world even faster if HBO were missing from their traditional pay TV packages. And, once HBO broke free from those pay TV ranks to go it alone, others followed in rapid succession. CBS, Showtime, Cinemax, Starz, TNT, Nickelodeon and a growing parade of others. Even slow-moving Viacom plans to join the SVOD club in 2018. Toward year-end 2017, CEO Bob Bakish teased an upcoming new service called "Phil" *(yes, that is that name that is being reported!)* at a monthly $20 price point. If Viacom is doing it, you know virtually everyone else is. Now the exception is not to *un*bundle.

The great unknown, of course, is how many stand-alone SVOD services or stripped down pay TV bundles the market can bear. After all, $15 here, $9.99 there – pretty soon consumers end up being at the same place they tried to escape from in the first place when they caught the cord-cutting bug.

And, a new major threat to HBO looms in the form of the SVOD cabal discussed in Chapter 4. HBO invented the Originals game "back in the day" to compete and win against traditional cable movie channels and broadcasters. But, now all the SVOD behemoths have stolen that Originals page from the HBO playbook *(more like the whole damn playbook!)*. The students have become the masters (or, at least peers), as high-cost, high production value Originals are the weapons of choice to win in our new Media 2.0 SVOD cage match.

So, with consumers awash in a sea of premium award-winning programming now from the likes of Netflix, Amazon, Hulu and others, even prestigious HBO feels the heat. And, it boasts a relatively meager $2 billion budget for its programming when compared to Netflix's $6 billion in 2017 ($7-$8 billion in 2018), Amazon's $4.5 billion, and even Hulu's $2.5 billion budgets for 2017.

Will AT&T fill HBO's Original coffers once it closes its Time Warner deal? According to HBO's CEO Richard Pieper, that won't be necessary. Speaking on CNBC in October 2017, he indicated that he has all that he needs. Quite a confident, contrarian view amidst the growing premium OTT video cacophony.

ESPN

Apart from HBO, ESPN of course will be another major stand-alone player in this hyper-competitive SVOD game once it launches its fully realized OTT sports vision. I already discussed ESPN at length in both Chapters 4 and 5. Feel free to revisit.

VICE

Vice is a different kind of digital-first media company – really more of an increasingly video-focused portal a la Yahoo! and AOL than a stand-alone OTT service (although it does offer video channels to other OTTs). Vice launched first as an underground print publication, but later fundamentally changed its stripes. If ESPN's new and soon-to-be significantly expanded SVOD is the jock, and HBO the artiste in the Media 2.0 video world, Vice is the rebel – the dangerous bad boy.

Vice launched "angry," featuring counter-culture, frequently shocking news stories that turned the traditional news world on its head. And it worked. The company's unprecedented middle finger-ian approach appealed to an entire generation of young millennials, many of whom felt nothing but apathy or even contempt for traditional news outlets. And, since Vice was where the coveted young audience was, Vice was where both Madison Avenue and Hollywood felt they needed to be. Even family-friendly Disney couldn't help itself, investing hundreds of millions of dollars in Vice over the past few years (which couldn't have been easy, given that Vice's form of storytelling isn't exactly told from *"The Happiest Place on Earth"*).

But then something equally unexpected happened. Vice put on its best suit and tie *(did we even know it owned one?)*, mellowed out, and launched a traditional linear channel on HBO in 2016. It chose the road less traveled – digital first, traditional television, second. That strategy worked – at least enough to attract a whopping $450 million cash infusion in 2017 from mega private equity firm TPG at an even more whopping $5.7 billion valuation, in order to accelerate Vice's own video-first and Originals strategy. According to CEO Shane Smith, Vice's goal right now is to create *"the largest millennial video library for content out there."*

So, after toying in late 2016 with the notion of filing for an IPO in 2017, Vice remains private for now.

That will change no later than 2019.

WWE NETWORK

Since we're talking about being bold and brash, how about bobbing, weaving and body-slamming? Professional "wrestling" (if you can call it that) SVOD service WWE Network is a surprisingly successful worldwide SVOD hit – with 1.63 million paying subscribers as of mid-2017. After all, a body-slam is a body-slam in any language, which means that the WWE Network's content travels well internationally. That's why these performers now find themselves in over 180 countries and announced in August 2017 that they will soon enter the ring in China with a major Chinese partner.

WWE's $9.99 monthly SVOD service proves that targeted specialized programming can be lucrative and succeed on an international scale.

VEVO

Music-focused Vevo is premium OTT video's privileged high school musician who gets accepted to Juilliard because of mommy and daddy's connections (Vevo shares similar pedigreed roots as its cousin, Hulu – i.e., big traditional media DNA). Two of the three major record labels own Vevo – Universal Music Group and Sony Music. The third, Warner Music, is not yet an actual owner, but finally did join the party in 2016 by licensing its music to Vevo for the first time. Like Hulu discussed earlier, Vevo used its parents' deep pockets to begin to spend aggressively in 2016 in order to be taken seriously as a premium OTT video contender.

Vevo has always been a free AVOD service like YouTube. Its user base is massive – about 100 million U.S. viewers watching 21.4 billion videos every month as of July 2017, and with 300 million more viewers internationally. But, in a little known fact (except to industry insiders), historically, over 90% of Vevo's traffic actually has come from YouTube. That means that YouTube first monetizes Vevo's content via advertising and gives back only a fraction to Vevo, although a better fraction than YouTube's typical 55% revenue split that it gives to video creators. Vevo must then give the lion's share of its fraction to the music labels and publishers (it says that it has paid our over $1 billion in royalties over time). That doesn't leave much for Vevo, which claimed about $500 million in revenues in 2016, a relatively small sum for a service that is so big. Not surprising, then, that it is widely understood that Vevo's economics are deeply challenged, a recurring theme for pure-play video services as we have seen.

In 2016, CEO Erik Huggers very publicly announced that Vevo would launch its own paid SVOD service later that year in order to accelerate its monetization path. But, that SVOD launch never happened, as Huggers slammed on the brakes to those ambitions in order to focus instead on international expansion. Huggers insists that Vevo's SVOD ambitions are *"completely still in the cards."* At least, that's his story, and he is sticking to it. Yet, even with its SVOD dreams on ice for now, Vevo continues to move forward to develop its own slate of mobile-first Originals that it hopes to monetize not only on its own service, but also across all social channels including Twitter, Snapchat and Instagram (you know, those without the YouTube middleman). Vevo's primary goal is to wean itself off its YouTube heroin addiction *(its mass traffic high)* and take back control of its own destiny in its bid to be profitable *(directly monetize its content so that it doesn't need to share with its pusher).*

Vevo's label parents are paying up big time right now for this rehab to at least slow down what they believe to be an increasing YouTube music menace *(I discuss this later in Chapter 13).*

SPOTIFY

Since we're talking music, we gotta talk Spotify, the world's biggest standalone music streaming service. *"But, Spotify isn't an OTT video streaming service,"* you insightfully say. Well, that was true up to 2016 when Spotify announced that it too was moving full throttle into the world of Originals. And it wasn't just talking good old-fashioned music videos at the time, but rather real, expensive premium scripted series. Sure, Spotify had featured clips from ESPN and others for quite some time, but these mobile-first Originals were announced as being a whole new direction.

As 2017 marched on, however, Spotify's video ambitions got fuzzy. Narrowed. Significantly. And at summer's end, Spotify's global head of content Tom Calderone exited the stage amidst new Spotify pronouncements that its once grand ambitions would re-focus on smaller, simpler videos for playlists brought to you by new content DJ Courtney Holt, former head of Maker Studios. Spotify undoubtedly realized that it would be virtually impossible for it to break through the collective noise of premium OTT video competition and dramatically change its audio stripes in our eyes *(er, more accurately ears)*. We use Spotify to listen. Would we really choose Spotify to satisfy our more video-centric urges in any meaningful way?

Quite a departure then, which became further apparent when Spotify announced a major strategic partnership with Hulu to deliver the premium video content it craved via a heavily discounted $5 per month premium audio/video bundle. Smart and savvy? Or just a sign of self-awareness and resignation that video will never play a leading role in Spotify's long-term strategy and must be content to be a supporting cast member? No matter what scale and scope, Spotify hopes that video will serve as some kind of meaningful differentiating and monetizing force that will lead it to profitability, a reality that continues to be far off in the distance as 2017 ended and as it approached its long-trumpeted IPO.

Stakes are extremely high. Place your bets on which services have a real chance of winning amidst this all-out premium OTT video war. Odds are long, and that list of winners will be short. But, at least these players are taking action.

Chapter 7

● ● ●

MOBILE-FIRST, MILLENNIAL-FOCUSED VIDEO COMPANIES (THE ARTISTS FORMERLY KNOWN AS "MCNS")

The earlier chapters laid out some of the leading big ticket video players in the premium motion picture and television-focused OTT video game, all of them backed by massive dollars or traditional media companies – and most *not* with a mobile-first millennial audience top of mind.

Now, let's move to the other side of the spectrum – the digital-first media companies that primarily feature mobile-friendly video content specifically targeted for a millennial audience (in other words, content for a generation growing up, looking down). These services most typically started in the world of ad-supported YouTube-ian user-generated content ("UGC").

Just a few years back, most of these new media companies were known as multichannel networks ("MCNs"). These were those quaint aggregators of YouTube channels that generally focused on a specific vertical audience or market segment. Their roots are fundamentally different from those of the major OTT video players discussed earlier.

I. FIRST, A WORD ABOUT MCNS

MCNs – that specific moniker and that specific aggregation "play" – were all the rage 3-4 years ago *(I wrote about them constantly myself)*. But, in the years since then, something curious happened. All of these digital-first video companies shied away from that acronym. Some, violently, contending they were never MCNs in the first place. And, they – at least the leading digital-first video companies that I discuss below – are right. The world in which they play (and how they play in it) has changed dramatically in a very short period of time.

MCNs are now a thing of the past. The successful ones are now simply new media companies focused on producing and distributing compelling mobile-first content that can be monetized in multiple Media 2.0 ways and across multiple platforms. Here's why.

First, the MCN business model simply didn't work. Initially, MCNs focused almost entirely on audience scale. Once that scale was achieved, virtually all category leaders turned to the question of revenue and chose an advertising-driven model to monetize their frequently hundreds of millions of subscribers (and for some, billion-plus). But, while that ad-driven strategy sounded so logical at the time, it never effectively monetized, especially since these new media companies also shared 45% of their ad revenues with YouTube.

And, because these MCNs had to monetize for themselves of course, they took their additional cut (typically 20-30%) from the remaining 55% and returned only the remaining fraction to their video creators. That made nobody happy – neither the MCN and its investors, nor the creators they represented who had significantly higher revenue expectations. And so, pure aggregation plays became suspect. On top of that, many creators who were not amongst the MCN's top-performers felt marginalized – that they were not getting the attention they deserved. That certainly didn't help. That's when, out of necessity, these companies pivoted. Some MCNs sooner than others.

Case in point, tween and teen-focused AwesomenessTV. This Media 2.0 video pioneer became the "poster child" for building a digital-first media company right. Early on in its life, AwesomenessTV stole a page from the HBO playbook *(sound familiar?)* and began to develop and distribute its own premium Originals, and it had the proven creative DNA chops and credibility to do it right. Then-CEO Brian Robbins came from the traditional media world and launched AwesomenessTV after he saw his kids obsessively watching animated videos on YouTube *(a perfect example of using your kids as your own personal Petri dish)*. AwesomenessTV poured significant resources into developing – rather than just aggregating – its own exclusive characters, content and special brand of storytelling. It also understood the value of building its own internal stable of video creators rather than relying primarily on the services of others.

And it worked. AwesomenessTV developed a compelling library of exclusive content, properties and characters that it exploited and monetized for big bucks in myriad ways, including licensing for movies and television. Add brand-funded and brand-integrated videos – so-called "branded content" or "content marketing" – and you had a powerful 1-2 punch that knocked down the former advertising-only model. Seeing AwesomenessTV's success amidst the existential economic challenges they faced, virtually all leading MCNs smartly followed suit. They, in essence, evolved simply into being digital-first production and distribution media companies that aspire to be their Awesome(nessTV) idol.

AwesomenessTV did another core strategic thing right. From the beginning, it proudly trumpeted its brand to the world. Yes, it developed and distributed multiple properties and built value in those sub-brands, shows and characters. But the company always placed the AwesomenessTV brand front and center. As a result, its audience knew precisely what it stood for – premium fun and safe kids content for a mobile-first world.

Many other "artists formerly-known-as-MCNs" *(an homage to Prince from a fellow Minnesotan)* didn't recognize this strategic imperative until much later. Several initially marketed their top individual creators and shows first, and their own brands second. This led to audience confusion. What kind of content did the company's brand stand for exactly? Audiences didn't really care. They simply wanted to watch the individual content titles they liked. And, that mattered to advertisers, potential distribution partners, and ultimately to investors. No surprise, then, that those MCNs that didn't build *their* brand first are doing much to change things now.

Finally, the term "MCN" simply no longer fits our ever-evolving Media 2.0 landscape. "Multichannel networks" literally meant companies that aggregated multiple YouTube – and essentially only YouTube – channels together in a subset under a different name. Well, guess what? It ain't a YouTube-only world anymore. Now we have Facebook, Snapchat, Twitter and a host of others that have become Media 2.0 companies themselves that are increasingly strategic to video creators and the former MCNs supporting them.

Welcome to our new multi-platform world where broad distribution and monetization are paramount. *(Speaking of Paramount, by the way, time to step up your Media 2.0 ambitions and be fearless – don't think you've been mentioned once in this book so far.)*

II. DIGITAL-FIRST MOBILE & MILLENNIAL FOCUSED VIDEO LEADERS

YouTube, of course, is the mother of all of these digital-first media companies, having birthed our entire UGC video world and getting paid handsomely for it with its 55/45 revenue split. As we have already seen, YouTube is almost everywhere millennial viewers want to be (music, sports, fashion, beauty, comedy, cats – *lots of cats* – you name it). But, its tremendous breadth is also its principal weakness. It is frequently challenging to navigate its ever-deepening ocean of content and ever-proliferating number of brands (YouTube "classic," YouTube Red, YouTube TV, not to mention all of the relevant Google offshoots like Google Play).

Here are some of the biggest and boldest new mobile-first and millennial-focused media companies that aim to solve YouTube's challenges. All have achieved significant scale, most are still primarily ad-supported, and most now have big name traditional media investors behind them – established players that frequently invest to learn more about the digital-first new media world and "try before they buy" (since strategic investors frequently become buyers as they get more confidence in a new unfamiliar space).

A. AWESOMENESSTV – THE POSTER CHILD

You already knew this one would be first on my list, given its pioneering Media 2.0 role. AwesomenessTV launched in 2012 and soon became one of the first highly successful and highly targeted digital-first media companies, hoping to build a better mousetrap in an increasingly mobile-first world *(pun intended in connection with my Disney/Maker Studios discussion below)*. And when it did, Gen Z tweens and teens came to the party, happily led by their exhausted parents who got some much-needed peace because of it.

DreamWorks Animation took notice and ultimately bought the company in 2013. Kudos to Jeffrey Katzenberg for being amongst the first traditional media execs to understand that the world had changed and he needed to get on board. And, because Comcast NBCUniversal swallowed up Dreamworks Animation for $3.8 billion in 2016, the Peacock now counts ownership in AwesomenessTV in its pecking order, together with joint-owners Verizon and digitally-evolving Hearst (both of which had made investments of their own in AwesomenessTV just before the sale which, suffice it to say, makes for "strange bedfellows" (*by the way, does anyone use that phrase anymore?*). So, Katzenberg's early action paid off big time. What cost him about $115 million back then is understood to have cost NBCUniversal about 4X that as part of its overall DreamWorks Animation deal only three years later. Not a bad Media 2.0 return on investment.

AwesomessTV says it takes a holistic approach to its storytelling, which is smart – very smart – because that represents the big Media 2.0 opportunity. President Brett Bouttier underscores that point, telling me that the company's *"biggest strength is making great content that is built to move across all types of media platforms, and an engaged audience that we are able to move to that programming on any platform."*

Creators, listen up. That's precisely how you should be thinking.

B. THE BROAD-BASED MOBILE-FIRST PLAYERS

These mobile-first video services try to cover extensive ground, not specifically focusing on any particular content, lifestyle or demographic market segment. Sometimes that works, but many times it doesn't due to an over-ambitious agenda versus giants with much deeper pockets.

MAKER STUDIOS

Maker Studios is first in this category of players because, up until 2017, it was one of the few digital-first media companies that covered multiple bases – not just one specific content category or market segment. Maker launched early 2009 and immediately became a juggernaut at least in terms of reach, if not in terms of compelling stand-alone economics. Video creators themselves made Maker (hence, the name), inspired by the story of traditional media's United Artists a long, long time ago and in a media galaxy far, far away. OTT video-inspired Disney bought Maker Studios in 2014 for what ultimately proved to be around $675 million (the deal had the potential to cost Disney up to $950 million with certain performance milestones). So, Maker has now been part of Disney's burgeoning Media 2.0 Magic Kingdom for several years.

Many scratched their heads when Disney opened its coffers wide to buy Maker. In fact, most scoffed. And they still do. Those nay-sayers felt vindicated in 2017 as virtually all of Maker's senior executives exited stage left, and Disney officially placed Maker into its Disney Digital division. Its new mission is to essentially exclusively focus on acting as a marketing and distribution engine for Disney-related franchises, movies, television and characters – which certainly wasn't a fundamental part of the original plan. Or, was it?

Buying Maker was never about stand-alone economics. Traditional media M&A metrics of revenue and EBITDA multiples were thrown out the window (just as they generally have been in all other major mobile-first media acquisitions to date). Rather, Maker's massive millennial and mobile footprint gave Disney an ability to reach a heads-down, mobile-focused generation of digital natives that it otherwise likely would not reach with its treasure trove of classic franchises, titles, characters and stories. And, that mega-marketing benefit alone may be enough to justify Maker's price tag, even if the going has been rough in these first few post-acquisition years.

CEO Bob Iger said as much when he announced the deal in the first place, underscoring that Disney primarily viewed Maker as being a distribution platform for the marketing of its storytelling. It's a basic point that is frequently lost on the deal's naysayers. A highly successful Maker-driven, mobile-centric, millennial-focused marketing campaign for one Disney mega-movie property alone (like *Star Wars*) holds the potential to generate hundreds of millions of incremental dollars at the box office (not to mention hundreds of millions more in all of Disney's ancillary channels and revenue streams). Do that a few times and the $675 million deal doesn't sound too bad, does it?

So, yes, these new digital-first, millennial-focused media companies face challenging stand-alone economics (although that is changing fast with new highly lucrative revenue streams that flow from content licensing and the production of Originals for major third-party OTT platforms). And, yes, early unanticipated M&A integration challenges muted Disney's and Maker's initial consolidated success. But, those significant challenges confront any party in M&A, and those realities do nothing to diminish the strategic value of the right digital-first new media company in the hands of the right, more traditional, strategic buyer that looks at the world with a much broader and longer-term ROI lens.

Evaluated in that light, Disney's acquisition of Maker still may prove to be a smart, savvy move. First, with one stroke of its pen, Disney entered the mobile-first, millennial-focused video world at mass scale and with the right DNA that Disney sorely needed to jump-start its Media 2.0 designs. To its credit, Disney humbly conceded to the world that it needed that DNA. Yes, most of those Maker execs have now left the building, but they undoubtedly made their (Maker's) mark *(a drink they still may be toasting to celebrate their M&A good fortunes)*. The Maker buy also sent a message both to Wall Street and Disney employees that its top brass took this brave new Media 2.0 world seriously. And, those signals matter. They set the tone. Impact culture.

I still like the deal.

STUDIO 71 (FORMERLY COLLECTIVE DIGITAL STUDIO)

Collective Digital Studio ("CDS") "suffered" a fate similar to Maker in 2015, selling to German-based media conglomerate ProSiebenSat.1, which then merged it into its leading German-based digital-first media company Studio71 in an overall deal valued at $240 million. CDS always had a relatively broad focus compared to most other mobile-first media companies, and is best known for its *Annoying Orange* series that it successfully monetized across multiple platforms, including television. So, CDS proved it could monetize. But, CDS never really built a consumer brand while doing it. ProSieben hopes to change that and use Studio71 as one of its secret weapons to penetrate the U.S. market.

Other European media giants joined ProSieben for this ride "across the pond" in 2017. France's leading commercial network TF1 and Italian broadcaster Mediaset together invested $56 million at a valuation that essentially doubled ProSieben's investment valuation less than two years earlier. *"Not bad for a nine-figure business,"* CEO Reza Izad tells me. He further points out that Studio71's growth rate since acquisition has been 65+% each year. According to Reza, *"1 in 3 Americans watch our content every month according to ComScore and we only have 900 U.S.-based channels. That is way less than Vevo and everyone else playing the scale game."* He then explains to me, *"This means Studio71 represents the largest number of hit channels on YouTube, Facebook, Instagram etc. out of all of our competitive set. Since we are in the culture business, that is really important and a significant distinction between us and the competition."*

Certainly Studio71 is one to watch in 2018 as it continues to raise its profile.

COMPLEX NETWORKS
This one is a 50-50 joint venture from our friends at Verizon and Hearst and promotes a broad-based "youth culture" focus *(whatever that means)*. Not surprisingly, given its Verizon DNA, Complex develops high-production (code for "expensive") mobile-first programming for the likes of Go90. It also produces and distributes content under its own brand across YouTube and other channels, boasting nearly 2 billion monthly video views in Q1 2017. One of its channels, *Rated Red,* is aimed at millennials in U.S. "red states," something sure to please a certain someone in the White House.

VESSEL
Scratch that one. Vessel's ship sailed over one year ago. The package broke. Verizon swallowed it up late 2016, shut it down, and integrated its technology.

See? Trying to cover too many bases is hard, especially when competing in a land of OTT giants.

C. TARGETED OR SO-CALLED "NICHE" CONTENT PLAYERS

And then there are the more focused mobile-first new media companies that cater to a specific underserved market segment with a specific category of content. But, don't kid yourselves. These so-called "niche" services, if done right, can add up to mass global audiences in our borderless OTT world. Doing it "right" in 2018, according to digital video pioneer and serial investor Allen DeBevoise, means that *"some of these vertical networks will focus on leveraging their brand and capabilities on the viral video super-platforms (e.g., YouTube, Facebook, Snapchat, Instagram) to pilot new formats and content IP for inclusion in their own OTT presence (part of next generation OTT bundles) or going direct to consumer via a freemium TVOD model for content in their category."*

Here are some of the ones worth knowing.

MACHINIMA

This young male and gamer-focused digital-first service initially launched years before the others in 2000, but really became the OTT video service we know today around 2009. Machinima quickly became one of the new MCN world's shining stars in terms of audience, both in its size and in its coveted young male demographic. Warner Bros. – keeper of the young male-focused DC Comics flame – invested $18 million early on as a result.

But the industry's reaction to Machinima was tepid at best for the past few years amidst grumblings of rocky monetization. And, although Warner Bros. invested an additional $24 million in 2015, it first passed on its option to buy Machinima in early 2016 and took a more "wait and see" attitude. That's when Machinima, like virtually all others I discuss in this chapter, heeded Media 2.0's *Jerry Maguire*-like call to *"Show me the money!"* And, in an homage to Maguire himself, Machinima's new mission statement became *"fewer clients (creators), more service (attention)."* That's why Machinima – surprise, surprise – went full throttle into its own Originals strategy in 2016.

And, that's when Warner Bros. finally made its move as 2016 ended, swooped in and – in true super-hero style – lifted Machinima to safety, bought the company, and gave it a logical new home in its DC Comics world. A collective sigh of relief could be heard from the Machinima faithful as final papers were signed, and the deal was sealed just in time for the holidays *(Thanksgiving indeed!)*. Perhaps not the best financial result, but a good result nonetheless. Sure beats the alternative.

STYLEHAUL

StyleHaul is a major mobile-first media brand that focuses on a market segment that is a world away from gamers – young millennial females who are interested in the fashion, beauty and lifestyle verticals. StyleHaul also launched fairly early on in the new mobile-first media world (2011) and broke out fast, aggregating thousands upon thousands of individual YouTube channels and creators (the company now counts over 23,000 of them). But, StyleHaul did what several others didn't – it told its own story well, thanks to charismatic founder Stephanie Horbaczewski. Stephanie enticed brands with the prospect of reaching a rabid audience smitten by YouTube stars who peddled fashion and beauty tips and the relevant products that go with them.

And, rabid that audience continues to be. In 2017, StyleHaul reached over 25 billion views on YouTube, 3.2 billion "likes," and nearly 50 million comments on Instagram. As a result of that kind of massive reach and passionate audience, StyleHaul achieved its own significant exit in 2014 when German media conglomerate Bertelsmann (via its RTL Group subsidiary) stepped up to take it out for $150 million after first being a major strategic investor *(see, try before you buy?).* So, StyleHaul's management team faces the same Disney/Maker Studios conundrum – great exit *(lots of cash and hot new Land Rovers)*, but now what? That's always the big question following an exit. How can the buyer keep the selling CEO happy and motivated to "win" after that CEO has already had his or her big pay day?

Here's the interesting part. Stephanie tells me that she is now more motivated than ever before – and I believe her *(yes, I know she is a great salesperson).* Here's why. First, StyleHaul now monetizes at significant scale. Stephanie tells me that they are *"trending and targeting over 9 figures in revenue"* for 2017. That means $100 million plus to you and me. And, that means StyleHaul is a real media company now. In Stephanie's words, *"It's big now. No joke."* Second, Stephanie effusively praises her RTL big media bosses for giving her and her team the best of both worlds. *"RTL is awesome. They are decentralized and let us run our own company. You get the stability and access of a big player with all the resources, but we are still very much acting like a startup."*

But, Stephanie is most excited about what's to come (as any good entrepreneur should be). And, what's to come in 2018 is to make so-called "graph theory" and machine learning central elements of StyleHaul's overall strategy. I could try to explain both concepts right now in deep technical detail. But, I won't. I'll spare you that fun. All you need to know is that StyleHaul will now use these two concepts together to tell brands, in the words of their new marketing materials, that they will generate *"more effective content campaigns by allowing brands and agencies to better select individual influencers and clusters of influencers, and by providing lucrative insight into the time-dependent evolution of successful campaigns."* Got that? Make sense? Well, Stephanie – who now describes herself as being a "data junkie" – says that these efforts mean that StyleHaul *"isn't just pressing against tomorrow, we're charging against it. It's that innovative."* Again, I believe her.

So, with all this OTT video excitement, why is RTL looking to sell StyleHaul's sister company BroadbandTV (something that it announced in 2017)? After all, BroadbandTV's scale is even more massive, generating 22 billion monthly impressions across 85,000 content creators. I ask Stephanie this question, and she tells me that she has *"no transparency"* into BroadbandTV's operations. But, she tells me that there is absolutely *"no way"* that RTL would even think of selling StyleHaul in 2018, or even after. *"They are incredibly bullish about the space and incredibly supportive."*

Will be interesting to analyze StyleHaul's lab results in 2018.

CRUNCHYROLL

Crunchyroll is all anime, all the time – 25,000-plus episodes of the best-licensed programming Asian media producers can offer. And, this Sensei serves a massive audience that eats it up. Voraciously. Most view for free, but the service also offers two paid tiers (monthly $6.95 and $11.95) for those who desire significantly more wasabi.

Berkeley college grads rolled Crunchyroll much earlier than most in 2006, and always focused on Asian-produced content for an audience primarily outside Asia. The Chernin Group of Fullscreen fame *(discussed earlier in Chapter 4)* bought a controlling interest in 2013 and then later contributed that stake to its Otter Media joint venture with AT&T. Crunchyroll now finds itself as an individual branded service under Otter's "Ellation" umbrella brand.

Otter Media's President Sarah Harden tells me that Crunchyroll is *"on fire"* and has not, like most other mobile-first new media services, *"suffered from 2017's Adpocalpyse"* (that is no typo, by the way – that is the term she used, and I think I know what it means). As I scratched my head wondering how a primarily free service could be killing it, Harden explained that Crunchyroll's parental brand, Ellation, is *"all about building identity brands with multiple revenue streams and built around emotional connection."* In other words, passionate communities characterized by what Harden calls *"brand love"* – which, for any capitalist, is the best kind of love out there.

Harden's test for whether any service has succeeded in building that kind of loving feeling with its fans is whether they become brand loyalists who show up at brand-sponsored live events, wearing the brand's t-shirts. If they do, then brand love translates not only into advertising and subscription dollars, but also into live event and merchandising revenues. And, Harden tells me that those somewhat "under the radar" revenue streams are substantial for Crunchyroll, as well as for other Ellation brands like Rooster Teeth.

So, taking Harden at her word, it appears that The Chernin Group/AT&T Otter Media union has produced a beautiful child or two indeed.

TASTEMADE

The innovators behind early short-form video pioneer Demand Media launched this foodie and travel-focused digital-first media company in 2012. Consider it a millennial and mobile-focused version of The Food Channel, with a healthy dose of Travel Channel sprinkled in. In fact, The Food Channel's majority owner, Scripps Networks (now owned by Discovery Communications), is a significant Tastemade investor, which ultimately makes it a very possible buyer.

Like AwesomenessTV, Tastemade carries one of the strongest Media 2.0 names and reputations amongst traditional media executives. Here's why. First, much like AwesomenessTV, Tastemade focused first on developing its own Originals and building a library of evergreen content that it could license and monetize over and over again. It was never just an aggregation play. Second, like AwesomenessTV, Tastemade always built its brand first and the brands of its creators second. That meant that its audience and potential distribution partners knew what Tastemade content represent-ed. Third, because of those two strategic pillars, Tastemade successfully achieved significant distribution across multiple key platforms like Apple TV much earlier than most – and broad-based distribution is the name of the game in our multi-platform world, remember?

Apart from its content, Tastemade's fundamental difference from AwesomenessTV is the fact that it is still a "hasn't-been-bought-yet" Indie, which is a bit surprising at this point. Undoubtedly, several have tried, but lofty valuation expectations likely roadblocked those deals. So, like all other independent digital-first media companies on this list, Tastemade's existential challenge is to effectively monetize at scale and, therefore, jus-tify its $80 million in financing to date and its long-term stand-alone story.

One of the most tantalizing possibilities here, apart from branded content, is video-driven e-commerce that should generously flow from this particu-lar food and travel market segment. Just think about it. You watch your favorite chefs. You see what they use to make their (and soon to be your) favorite recipes. And, bam! Up comes an instant, seamless buying oppor-tunity with a tension-inducing time limit. Of course you'll buy!

But, that tasty potential hasn't been cooked up yet in any big way. And, word on the street is that the company is ready to sell, something I fully expect will happen in 2018 latest *(okay, maybe 2019 … but not later than that!)*.

WHISTLE SPORTS

Whistle Sports launched in 2014 to bring a new and very different kind of sports-related entertainment to an audience that they split into so-called "digital natives" (26-34 year olds who watch across platforms) and "social natives" (13-25 year olds who don't just watch, they lean in and actively engage). Rather than traditional sports, Whistle focuses on millennial-invented eSports, basketball dunking, slack-lining, and bottle tossing – all of which are a world away from ESPN. And that's the point. In CEO John West's words, *"Today's generation is developing new formats: authentic commentary, behind-the-scenes, comedic sports, trick shots, etc. They are also combining sports with pop culture and music, taking down the adult-created walls between genres and creating their own amazing, entertaining and inspiring video content."*

So, while Whistle won't bring Chris Berman to your living room TV, it *"will, go, all, the, way!"* to bring trick-shot basketball stars "Dude Perfect" – and 500 other curated video creators – to your mobile screens. Whistle counts an audience of more than 400 million (as of October 2017) who watch 1.5 billion videos monthly across all platforms. And, West tells me that the company is on track to join the *"$100 million revenue club"* in the 2018-2019 time frame.

Whistle's strengths? First, its impressive war chest and the strategic media players who bankrolled it. The company expanded its Series C financing round to $27.5 million in 2017, bringing its total haul to well over $70 million – a sum that includes major investments from global sports powerhouses Sky and Liberty Global, as well as a small strategic infusion from Jeffrey Katzenberg's WndrCo as the year ended. If these international media giants fully embrace Whistle's vision, global coverage is in its reach. Second, the company is a biz dev machine, cranking out impressive licensing wins with virtually all major professional sports leagues, big-budget content deals with Go90 and others, and a fast-growing slate of lucrative branded content deals.

Whistle's challenges? The same as most others on this list – effectively monetizing its content across multiple distribution channels, developing Originals for other OTT services at scale and, in West's words, *"constantly re-imagining our company to remain relevant to today's generation."* Sound familiar? It's a recurring theme. Whistle hopes that a new strategic focus in 2018 on direct-to-consumer monetization via multiple pathways – "TVOD" (transactional video on demand, where you only pay for what you watch), SVOD, AVOD, live events, merchandising – will help bring them to the promised land.

Given all that it has going for it (category leader in the coveted millennial sports segment, and sports-focused global strategic investors who understand their need to reach those millennials), Whistle – like Tastemade – will not retain its Indie status for long. It's merely a question of who, what valuation, and when.

I'll use that 2018-2019 timeframe again here.

IZO (FORMERLY DANCEON)

Originally focused on dance alone when it launched in 2010, this digital-first media company changed its name to IZO in 2016 to underscore that it had broadened its focus beyond dance to music in general. After all, this is the company credited with unleashing Silento's *Nae Nae* craze loose to the world *(is that a good thing?)*. That's its star-making potential, and IZO now counts itself amongst the top 5 brands for music online (top 2 for teens).

IZO's marquee investors include Nygel Lythgoe (of *Dancing with the Stars* and *American Idol* fame) and Madonna (yes, the Material Girl herself). IZO's CEO Amanda Taylor tells me that her focus for 2018, together with Lythgoe (an active investor), will be to *"leverage its brand, audience and content capabilities to produce and distribute premium programming"* in all flavors. That means unscripted reality series, docu-series that profile major music artists, scripted series, and musical narratives.

Surprisingly, given its attention-seeking investor roots, IZO flies "under the radar," and its key challenge is to sing (not just dance) its own praises more loudly. But, I have always liked this music and dance category and company. Music alone is by far the single most popular content category online, driving 40+% of YouTube's video views. And, IZO's infectious content combo of music and dance is truly global and universal, not bogged down by any language barrier.

IZO too will find a home – perhaps in strategic investor AMC Entertainment.

JUKIN' MEDIA

These guys are just different. In a good way. Jukin' is the quintessential bootstrapped start-up. Its founder, Jon Skogmo, started with an idea and an apartment. Jukin' has taken in significantly less cash than others, but is a rare profitable player in this space. The company launched early on in this digital-first game (2009) and initially focused almost-exclusively on highly viral so-called "fail" videos *(you know, those ones where a skateboarder slides down a rail, falls and lands on his crotch?)*. Not particularly highbrow perhaps, but extremely effective and, importantly, global. As Skogmo likes to say, *"a fail is a fail in any language"* after all. And so, Jukin's brand stands for something – failure (in fact, the company's office features a sign that reads *"Failure is the Only Option!"* … you gotta love that!).

Jukin' Media, unlike most others, still believes in UGC. Skogmo tells me, *"we believe the future of storytelling is user generated. We discover and acquire everyday stories told by everyday people."* So, Jukin' started from that foundation and built up its expertise to efficiently spot and acquire those UGC videos that showed signs of virality, adding its own "special sauce" to accelerate that growth. And it worked. The company now owns a deep library of UGC content that it monetizes in multiple ways, including lucrative licensing deals. You know those cringe-worthy clips you see on *Tosh.O*? Yup, those are from Jukin.'

Jukin' reports 60 million subscribers and 1 billion monthly views across four individual brands as of July 2017. That impressive growth led Skogmo and his team to find a new physical home for its expanding business in LA, as well as new homes overseas in London and Australia. So, what are Jukin's greatest hurdles for continued success in 2018? According to Skogmo, *"the biggest risks to our business are internal, not external. There is an extreme amount of focus that is required and we want to make sure that we are focusing on the right opportunities as opposed to chasing shiny objects."* In other words, things he can control, rather than the things he can't, like the actions of others.

My prediction is that Jukin' will find a new ownership home within a large strategic buyer in 2018, or 2019 at the latest. Several have tried and failed so far. But, the timing just feels right at this point.

KIN COMMUNITY

You can think of Kin Community (founded in 2011) as being a humbler and softer-spoken version of StyleHaul – a digital-first video service for women, rather than tween and teen girls. But, even in its far more stealthy and mysterious ways, Kin Community amassed over $40 million in financing over time. Kin's older female demographic is both a marketing blessing and a curse. Its core audience holds significantly more real "here and now" purchasing power. But, advertisers increasingly covet always-on mobile-focused and younger millennial eyes.

Kin's Achilles heel is its overall discipline and humility (as if those are bad things … although they sometimes can be in our increasingly aggressive Media 2.0 world). The company studiously focuses first on ongoing profitability *(imagine that?)* and historically sacrificed scale because of it. That major challenge, however, presents Kin's most significant opportunity – to expand its profile and break out from its "under the radar" status. It will attract more brand-name partners if it celebrates itself more. Otherwise, it risks staying small, which is okay if that's the way CEO Michael Wayne and company want it.

But, institutional investors – whom Wayne now counts as kin – rarely do. Scratch that. Never do. Wayne now must listen to their advice, then, at the dinner table.

UPROXX MEDIA (FORMERLY WOVEN DIGITAL)

Much like Kin is a kindler, gentler version of StyleHaul, Uproxx Media (formerly Woven Digital) positions itself as being a "friendlier" version of Vice. The company still tells marketers that it, like Vice, is millennial male-focused. But it now takes active strides to expand its core base, which former Executive Chairman Colin Digiaro told me reached 40% women as 2016 closed. Uproxx also has raised significant sums – in its case, $40 million. It's great to have all that cash, of course, but that moolah also means that Uproxx, like Kin, faces more pressure than ever before from its institutional investors to scale and monetize profitably.

Originals, yet again, are the strategy of choice to confront that challenge and for Uproxx to accomplish its mission. But, also expect the company to increasingly focus on building its new overall brand and landing impactful new multi-platform distribution deals. You know, kind of like what all the others need to do.

CRYPT TV

Crypt TV is a relatively new mobile-first media company that, as its name rather obviously suggests, focuses on the horror genre. Crypt TV appropriately comes from the minds of scare-meister Jason Blum (investor) and *Hostel* director Eli Roth, together with CEO Jack Davis. I love this genre for mobile/millennial ADD appetites. First, compelling scary storylines can come in bite-sized, mobile-friendly packages and surface in minutes. Second, those short ghost stories frequently don't require much dialog and, therefore, travel well because "a scare is a scare in any language." Third, good frights – just like cute pets – are extremely viral. We share them incessantly.

Finally, and perhaps most intriguingly, short scares and new meme-worthy viral characters lend themselves to much longer treatment ultimately in movies and television, not to mention central roles in live events and merchandising – all of which mean licensing cha-ching! Our small screens, in effect, become test grounds for the much larger and more lucrative screens, where short stories and proven characters cost-effectively come to life in full big screen glory and with a built-in thrill-seeking mass audience ready to spend.

Jason Blum already cracked the code for making hit after hit in the theatrical horror movie world. With his active involvement, I like Crypt TV's chances for the small screen. The potential here to develop a holistic multi-platform and highly monetizing media company is downright scary … in the best possible way.

D. TARGETED DEMOGRAPHIC-FOCUSED SERVICES

MITU

Like AwesomenessTV, traditional media executives launched Mitu in 2012 with a Latino audience in mind *("By Latinos, for Latinos"* was the way founder and original CEO Roy Burstin first described his vision). Burstin stepped down late 2017 when long-time media exec Herb Scannell took over, but he had already expanded Mitu's vision well before, telling me that Mitu strives to be the home of mainstream multi-cultural content for an audience he calls *"the 200%"* – that is, content that has *"100% connection with American culture, and 100% with heritage cultural value."*

Mitu has raised $43 million to date from investors that include advertising agency giant WPP. Its vote of confidence demonstrates how significant that brand-focused Media 2.0 market opportunity is, especially since, according to Burstin, *"Latinos have the most diverse social footprints."* Not surprising, then, that Facebook is Mitu's single most important platform – its *"home base."* And, that social footprint can be a marketing goldmine. Marketers, are you getting the point here? That's the opportunity, and all of these digital-first media companies are hungry to work with you.

Like all independent digital-first new media companies, Mitu faces significant challenges in a sea of giants, including overall monetization and profitability at scale. Lionsgate, for example, is reaching out to the U.S.-based Latino market with its new Spanish language OTT service "Pantaya," although its Spanish language-centric approach is quite different than Mitu's primarily English-driven cross-cultural content approach.

Let's see where Mitu's new CEO takes things in 2018. Undoubtedly, Scannell's traditional big media and brand-connected roots offer clues.

ALL DEF DIGITAL

All Def Digital, like Mitu, also focuses on a market that many main-streamers still believe is "niche" – hip hop and youth culture (traditionally referred to as "urban"). But, traditional media, wake up! Hip-hop continued to be at the center of the entertainment universe in 2017 (witness HBO's brilliant *The Defiant Ones* series featuring Dr. Dre and Jimmy Iovine, Kendrick Lamar's chart-topping album *Damn.*, and the continuing dominance of *Hamilton* on Broadway as just three examples across different platforms). Sanjay Sharma, who stepped down as CEO late 2017 but remains on the board, emphasizes to me that *"millennial and Gen-Z hip hop is a movement that transcends race ethnicity, socio-economic class, gender and geography."* And, he is absolutely right.

Russell Simmons launched All Def in 2013, and this "mini"-OTT now reaches over 6 million fans and subscribers that drive nearly 300 million monthly views of its Originals (as of October 2017). The company has scored $18 million of financing to date to become hip-hop's answer to

Vice. Significantly, leading Silicon Valley blue-chip venture capital firm Andreessen Horowitz invested in its last round, underscoring that the Northern California Silicon Valley-based tech world now finally takes the Southern California content-driven world seriously *(as it should)*. That's no small feat. After all, media and tech are two great tastes that taste great together. That's Media 2.0.

Sharma tells me that All Def's primary areas of focus for 2018 *"are, from a content genre point of view, fueling growth in music-related programming, and continuing to expand new vertical entries in both social justice and sports."* And, further, *"from a business model point of view, we will continue our strategy of driving audience growth on short-form social platforms with huge engagement, but double down on success we've had in 2017 with premium programming across television, film and premium digital platforms."* All Def, like essentially all other digital-first media companies discussed in this chapter, also will continue to scale out their brand partnerships. Its biggest risks in 2018? Apart from focus, Sharma stoically tells me that *"competition from much more established players like Vice and Oath"* is a significant one.

That's a central issue that faces all niche/segment-focused OTT video players as they battle much more significantly resourced players for mind and market share.

88 RISING

88 Rising is another demographic-focused new multi-platform media company. Its founders tell me that it focuses on pan-Asian millennial-friendly content from creators across multiple Asian territories. The company, based in New York City, closed its first significant round of financing in 2017, led again by WPP and including Alan DeBevoise's Third Wave Digital fund, as well as my very own SAM CREATV Ventures fund. So, obviously I am a believer.

88 Rising features and represents some of Asia's top young social media influencers and musical artists who already have extensive global reach. And, most intriguing, the company already holds deep relationships with global brands and is known for its high-end production chops. That means both lucrative branded content and premium video and related IP that it can license to others across multiple platforms.

Mitu, All Def Digital and 88 Rising – three different services that play to three different underserved markets.

E. INTERNATIONAL MOBILE-FIRST NEW MEDIA PLAYERS

A word about the global mobile-first new media marketplace. It's already massive, with literally hundreds of players of varying shapes and sizes. But, for the sake of logistical necessity as I write this book – not to mention my own mental and physical health – I have essentially focused this chapter exclusively on U.S.-based players.

To give you at least a taste of what's hidden beyond U.S. borders – size, scope and opportunity – check out Vietnam-based "Yeah1 Network." I bet you never heard of it, and I bet you are thinking right now to yourself that Vietnam is a market so small that you should just skip over this section. But hold on. Check this out.

Yeah1 is a broad-based mobile-first, youth-focused media company that strangely still calls itself an MCN (one of the few that still embraces that label), aggregates thousands of channels, counts 4 billion monthly video views (90% from within Vietnam) and – here's the best part – claims to be highly scaling, monetizing and profitable. How can that be? Well, CEO Brian Tiong tells me that Yeah1 caters to a mobile-exclusive consumer base where only 5% of the population carry pay TV subscriptions. So, they are hungry for its small screen-focused ad-supported videos.

Yeah1 hopes to take its winning formula across Southeast Asia, with kids programming leading the way.

And, that's just Yeah1.

So many territories. So few pages to cover them.

F. DIGITAL-FIRST STUDIOS

NEW FORM DIGITAL

New Form Digital – from traditional media's dynamic duo of Ron Howard and Brian Grazier – also is a different kind of digital-first media player (and not just because of its royal Hollywood pedigree). Founded in 2014, New Form makes no pretenses of being anything more than a digital-first production company that produces premium high quality content for Media 2.0 distribution platforms and brands that are willing to pay top dollar for it. New Form underscored this pure studio approach in 2017 when it publicly confirmed that it would drop all plans to distribute its own Originals across its own social media platforms, so that it could focus 100% on selling its stories directly to buyers.

And, those buyers are buying. New Form already produces multiple multi-million dollar web series for multiple OTT players, including Verizon's Go90, YouTube Red and Fullscreen. Some industry observers are skeptical of a production company's ability to scale its creative services. But, New Form's COO JC Cangilla tells me that the team has worked to build a *"full-service studio that can scale over time, much like any of the great digital businesses based out of Silicon Valley."* He and his team continue to prioritize creating great content, of course, for 2018. But, other key priorities include working more closely with marketers and brands (a theme voiced by all digital-first video companies) and pursuing more opportunities in the international marketplace. Amen to that.

Assuming New Form can continue to spot and develop strong stories, scale its production services, and keep its related economics in check (three tall orders to be sure), then it is well-positioned within this hyper-competitive, Originals-driven digital marketplace. All distributors of all stripes increasingly need compelling, differentiating exclusive content in order to effectively compete.

New Form has established itself as a leading digital brand to make that happen.

WNDRCO/NEW TV

I told you earlier that Jeffrey Katzenberg would be back, and here he is (and not in a small way, of course). In 2017, Katzenberg announced his latest new media company WndrCo with great fanfare and with $600 million in initial financing. His vision is to both incubate and buy digital-first media companies a la fellow traditional media mogul Barry Diller and IAC.

WndrCo's first incubated company is "New TV" which, in many ways, acts a lot like good old-fashioned old TV – that is, high-end primetime TV-like storytelling from A-list top-line and bottom-line talent (*in other words, expensive!*) – only in smaller increments to suit an audience of 18-34 year old mobile natives. Katzenberg plans to spend as much as $125,000 per minute for episodes that last no longer than 10 minutes, but are intended to feature what he describes as *"full story arcs."* That's why he now looks to raise a jaw-dropping $2 billion more to fuel New TV and develop a critical mass of initial programming. That cash stash most likely will come from a mega-distribution partner who shares Katzenberg's somewhat "throw-back-ian" view of the media world – and who, like Katzenberg, sees no room for ads to pollute that high-end vision and, instead, plans to use title sponsorships and brand integrations to pay for it all.

New TV certainly represents a contrarian blueprint to the Media 2.0 world, and execs across both old and new media scratched their heads when it was first announced. While others like international digital-first production studios Studio+ and Blackpills somewhat share New TV's luxury high-end vision, their overall economics are substantially more modest *(for its part, in Q4 2017, Vivendi's Studio+ proudly trumpeted 5 million subscribers to its mobile-first premium content across the likes of Orange in France, TIM in Italy, and Vivo in Brazil)*.

Will Media 2.0 lightning strike twice for this legend? Or will New TV's more traditional Media 1.0-ish economics and overall ethos strike it down?

Place your bets now.

G. IT'S A WRAP

Other intriguing players in this digital-first, mobile-focused video space abound. These include both startups like little known *(but deserving to be known)* multi-lingual health, wellness and news-focused "Natcom Global" (which produces premium content in Spanish, English and Portuguese – and still does it all profitably, imagine that?), and startup "RatherBe" (which focuses on the active and outdoor lifestyle and integrates community and commerce, elements too frequently ignored by most). They also include new mobile-first services from the big boys, like Warner Bros.' "Stage 13" that features content that spans horror, comedy and drama. And, of course, scores of others – including mini-giants BuzzFeed (itself rumored to be eyeing an IPO in 2018) and Vox Media – increasingly and smartly focus on video, the new universal language of our times.

Traditional media and entertainment executives should actively study and court all of these leading players that remain independent. Many of them will not retain their Indie status by the end of 2018 (or 2019 at the latest) due to ever-increasing hyperactivity in the overall Media 2.0 space.

Chapter 8

●　●　●

TRADITIONAL MEDIA'S DIGITAL-FIRST REALITY CHECK (AND M&A MISSION)

Speaking of M&A, consolidation continued to be a headline story in 2017. AT&T marched onward in 2017 to close its $85 billion acquisition of Time Warner, and Verizon closed its deflated acquisition of Yahoo! with a final price tag of $4.48 billion. Meanwhile, pay TV giant Discovery Communications acquired Scripps Network Interactive (owner of HGTV, Food Network, and Animal Planet) for $11.9 billion. These are massive bets placed by mega-players (telcos, cable conglomerates) thirsty for exclusive differentiating premium content. Expect a continuing string of content-fueled Media 2.0-fueled M&A to follow in 2018 and beyond, especially since massive strategic deals spur competitors to take out remaining dance partners. You can bet that corporate development conference rooms are buzzing as we speak.

Now let's take a look at M&A by the major media and entertainment companies themselves, the targets of which frequently are Chapter 7's digital, mobile-first media companies. These deals are driven by traditional media's need to expand into the Media 2.0 content space. It took a while – in fact, it continues to take too much of a while for many major media and entertainment companies – but several "big fish" now finally understand that the world in which they play has transformed radically with the onset of truly smart phones and the increasingly-speedy wireless networks that feed them.

It shouldn't have been that hard though. All these traditional executives had to do was look around and see where the kids are – increasingly heads down obsessed at the small screen inches in front of them. And, if that's where the kids are, then that's where you gotta be, including the marketers that want to reach them. Once this reality is accepted, then traditional media and entertainment companies have three choices to get there. Build. Partner. Or buy.

The smart ones recognized that it would take too long to build, and further that they didn't have the right Media 2.0 human DNA to do it right anyway. After all, for the most part, young millennial talent built and launched these leading digital-first media companies to reach an audience that looked like them. That left either partnering (most typically in the form of strategic investment, as discussed in Chapter 7) or buying.

Several went all-in and bought. As discussed earlier, DreamWorks Animation really started it all in 2013 when it acquired AwesomenessTV. But, that was nothing compared to Disney's shot across the bow in 2014 when it bought Maker Studios for the deal that ultimately valued it at $675 million. A long litany of M&A followed Disney's aggressive move. As we have seen, Otter Media snapped up Maker's primary competitor, Fullscreen. Bertelsmann subsidiary RTL Group swallowed up StyleHaul. German media conglomerate ProSiebenSat.1 bought Collective Digital Studio and merged it into its own Germany-based MCN Studio71.

And that's the fundamental point. Companies use M&A to transform themselves in ways unique to each situation – to enter a new market, buy needed assets, accelerate growth, instantly recruit the right DNA, send a message of innovation to the Street, and also frequently simply to keep that asset out of the hands of competitors. Don't underestimate the power of M&A defensive motivations.

That's why most of the remaining Indie category leaders will be bought in the next 2-3 years – most likely by one of their major traditional media company strategic investors.

Just a question of how much and when.

Chapter 9

• • •

ALL MEDIA IS SOCIAL
(OR IS IT THE OTHER WAY AROUND?)

Remember the mobile "second screen" talk of yore? Well, it ain't second screen time anymore. Mobile is now the first screen, especially for millennials who share everything they see. That means that all media is – or at least has the potential to be – social. And that reality presents a massive opportunity for content creators and the social platforms that support them. Those two notions of "social" and "media" are intertwined.

That's why Facebook and the other leading social media companies – no longer content to simply serve as our connective tissue in this Media 2.0 age – have transformed themselves into full-fledged new mega-media companies in literally just the past couple years. Now, as we have seen, these social animals have their sights set on developing and distributing their own premium Originals to differentiate themselves from the others, acquire and retain users, deepen their overall engagement and relationship with those users, and more effectively monetize them.

Does this content-driven strategy sound familiar? Sounds a lot like the major OTTs and digital-first media companies that they increasingly target.

But, the fundamental difference, of course, is that these guys already have the increasingly strategic community piece nailed.

Here are the major social Media 2.0 players.

FACEBOOK

As discussed at length in Chapter 4, Facebook made massive investments in both premium VOD and live streaming these past two years to take YouTube head-on. While Facebook's monetization path remains unproven, the engagement part doesn't. Media 2.0 companies saw massive numbers and audience growth on Facebook in 2017, and that was even before it launched its new "Watch" premium TV-like programming service. That's why creators and marketers are taking notice. Now, virtually all digital-first media companies actively court Facebook distribution – and, voila, YouTube has its first real threat. From the sounds of it *(and my ears are pretty close to the ground)*, YouTube feels it, and is smartly accelerating its own innovation and experimentation because of it.

Facebook's sheer size and scope are its greatest strengths. It has the financial wherewithal to do just about anything it wants and expand its reach in ways unavailable to most. To a certain extent, the same can be said about archrival YouTube of course. But, we – the reported 2 billion-plus monthly active users as of June 2017 – engage with Facebook far more actively than with YouTube. For many of us, it is woven into the fabric of our daily, if not hourly, lives. Check this out – 50% of Facebook's 1.3 billion-plus active daily users go to Facebook even before brewing their first cup of coffee each morning.

Facebook also collects significantly more detailed information about each of us than do YouTube and others *(Amazon excluded)*, because we so happily share it. That puts Facebook in a good position to know what content speaks to us as individuals which, in turn, means deeper engagement and potentially deeper monetization.

Facebook's biggest challenge is focus. This juggernaut is so many different things, including Instagram and virtual reality (VR) pioneer Oculus. Its sheer mass also hinders its accelerating media ambitions. Traditional media companies are wary of giving away too much of their prized premium content for fear of losing control, kind of like they are with Apple. To regain their trust, Facebook has introduced new monetization initiatives to benefit frequently struggling, traditional players. One 2017 example includes a new pay wall subscription model a la *The New York Times* to access premium publisher content.

"Watch" Facebook closely in 2018. You can bet that YouTube and the others will.

INSTAGRAM

Instagram is Facebook's child, enabling its core tween and teen audience to connect and communicate via images and video. Facebook acquired Instagram in 2012 for $1 billion and significantly expanded its video focus in 2017. COO Marne Levine underscored that point mid-year when she reported that Facebook and Instagram users spend 50% more time watching videos and create four times more videos than they did in 2016.

Instagram competes directly with Snapchat of course (which Facebook tried to buy earlier, by the way), and Snapchat led the way with social video at scale. But, here's Instagram's special power – it is shameless. Instagram makes no bones about the fact that it is willing to replicate *(okay, let's just say it because Instagram's CEO Kevin Systrom did, "copy")* Snapchat's success. Instagram "Stories" anyone? And, get this – Instagram Stories passed 250 million daily active users by mid-2017 *(repeat, just for Stories)*, while

Snapchat's total audience *(repeat, total)* reached 173 million (or about 2/3 that) in the same time period. Instagram's not-so-secret recipe for success against Snapchat is its very special place in the Facebook family and the privileges that flow from that. Facebook brings its connected friends list to Instagram, making it much easier for Instagram users to find and retain new followers than with Snapchat.

Kind of nice and efficient for Instagram to be able to use Snapchat as its product development team, don't you think? Instagram is more than happy to be the fast-follower to Snapchat's first-mover status.

SNAPCHAT
Speaking of Snapchat (the ghost-ian company that invented the great disappearing act for messages and images), parent company Snap successfully went public in 2017 in an IPO valued at nearly $24 billion. Snap's twin goals with its new cash hoard are to expand its base (get older) and monetize more (get richer) by attracting more TV-like ad dollars. To that end, Snapchat introduced "Snapchat Shows" in 2017, a companion to its existing "Discover" feature that launched one year earlier.

Discover, as you may recall, is Snapchat's gift to established new and old world content brands like *BuzzFeed, Cosmopolitan,* and *People.* It is essentially a velvet rope portal where invite-only content partners hold the coveted privilege of creating new branded content for an entirely new audience that they otherwise likely would never reach. Discover launched with a relative hodge-podge of initial content partners *(I scratched my head at the time about CNN's relevance to tweens and teens, as one example).* But, that fact alone demonstrated how experimental Discover was. Several major (and perhaps more obviously logical) media brands just didn't "get" it and chose not to participate at launch. Well, guess what? They are kicking themselves now because of it. That's the price of taking a traditional "wait and see" attitude in this Media 2.0 age.

This year's model, Snapchat "Shows," can be found in its "Stories" section and takes the service's video ambitions beyond Discover's branded channels approach. Snap's goal with "Shows" is to feature a broad range of compelling Originals *(yes, there's that strategy again)* – mobile-focused to be sure, but some scripted and with big budgets. This time, unlike how things were when Snap launched Discover, seemingly every major media and content brand wants to be along for the ride *(so long as that ride is vertical because, remember, that is the preferred video language of our horizontally-challenged millennial kids).*

NBCUniversal, as an example, invested $500 million in Snap's IPO and increasingly invests in developing high-end episodic shows exclusively for SnapChat, including bite-sized versions of existing hit shows (*Saturday Night Live, The Voice*) and entirely new Originals like twice-daily NBC News show *Stay Tuned* (which generated 29 million unique viewers in less than one month after its July 2017 launch). NBCUniversal took things even further late 2017 when it announced a 50/50 joint venture with Snap to produce mobile-first scripted series. Not to be outdone, Time Warner handed Snapchat $100 million in cash to develop ten mobile-first Originals for its ADD audience. And now most other media giants are following suit (including ABC, BBC, Turner, Scripps, ESPN, Discovery and even the NFL) both for the "right" reasons (it's smart) and for some "wrong" ones (because everyone else is doing it).

Let's focus on being smart. Snapchat opens up tens of millions of young, obsessed daily users to those traditional shows and media brands. Many, for the first time. The great hope, of course, is for that massive promotional reach to pull Snapchat newbies into the more traditional television media fold and monetize them with more lucrative traditional media economics. Scripps' president of content distribution Henry Ahn lays it out plainly. *"Snapchat's distinctive mobile platform provides an ideal environment for us to touch millennials and centennials who may not yet be hooked on our premium offerings."* In other words, we don't have 'em, but we need 'em.

For those content creators like NBCUniversal and Time Warner that understand the basics of Media 2.0 and develop content specifically for Snapchat – rather than merely try to slice and dice existing content to make it fit – this grand experiment is paying off. And now Snapchat counts Madison Avenue and the piles of branded money flowing from it as close friends. That's the great part.

But, Snapchat is challenged. Big time. As we have seen, Snapchat's arch-nemesis is Facebook-backed Instagram. At first, Snapchat may have found Instagram's mimicking of its continuing string of powerful new differentiating features to be a little bit quaint *("Crowd Surf" was one of my 2017 favorites, giving music festival-goers a single multiple P.O.V. video experience from individual mobile phone streams stitched together in real-time with perfectly synchronized audio)*. Downright flattering. But, no longer. Instragram's all-out assault on Snapchat and its most successful features has taken its toll.

Snap investors approached the end of 2017 wary indeed after seeing early post-IPO warning signs, including Q2 2017's reality check that daily active users rose a mere 4% over Q1. As a result, Snap's lofty valuations dissipated like a dejected ghost following its IPO. Now, Snap investors must take solace in the fact that Facebook's stock dropped massively too in its first year post-IPO. That's when Facebook began to re-invent itself to become the multi-platform juggernaut it is today.

Can Snap emulate Facebook this time? It certainly won't be easy, since Snap's seemingly massive IPO capital infusion still represents only a small fraction of the resources at Facebook's disposal.

But, I am pulling for this LA-based innovator.

TWITTER

"Twitter a media company?" you ask. The answer – at least aspirationally – is most definitely "yes." That's why rumors swirled back in 2016 that Disney,

among others, had interest in buying it. Twitter has been the media and entertainment world's second-screen bestie for years, with hash tags filling our living room television screens. Entertainment companies aggressively use Twitter to promote their movies, television, and sports to an audience who demand to know "what's happening?" in the world right now. But, despite all the early morning Tweets bombarding us from the White House in 2017 *(who needs coffee to wake up anymore?)*, Twitter's growth stalled. And, the service somewhat shockingly attracted zero *(yes, 0!)* new customers as Q2 2017 ended.

That's why Twitter continued to signal its big media ambitions and make its own audacious content-fueled Media 2.0 moves in 2017, paying up massive dollars to buy exclusive streaming rights to premium live entertainment programming from the likes of Major League Baseball and the PGA Tour (although it lost out to Amazon for a second year of live streaming rights to NFL *Thursday Night Football*). As a result, its total hours of live content grew from 500 at the end of 2016 to 800-plus less than three months later.

Why focus on premium live content? Because despite its global mass reach and central place in the global *Zeitgeist*, Twitter must monetize more effectively and demonstrate to the Street that it is more than the sum of its 140 individual parts. Twitter is betting on streaming major live events to be its salvation.

So, are you ready for some football, I mean, baseball?

LINKEDIN
Microsoft owns LinkedIn after it paid a whopping $26.2 billion in 2016 to acquire it in its own audacious Media 2.0 move. By now, you would kind of expect video to be front and center in the LinkedIn experience. Seems logical, right? But, look again *(you probably check it daily anyhow)*. Barely any video content in sight, and that didn't change much in 2017.

I continue to believe that LinkedIn has a green field game-changing opportunity to integrate video deeply into our overall user experience, including via both professionally produced video (business and financial news) and more personal business videos (video profiles and testimonials). And, as video increasingly seeps into its world, expect LinkedIn to increasingly compete with other OTT video players. That's why I include it here. Maybe a bit of a curve ball, but they can't all be right down the middle.

SO MANY MORE SOCIAL CREATURES, SO LITTLE TIME

So many others to discuss. Take Musical.ly, the wildly successful music video lip-syncing app. Musical.ly announced its own major studio partnerships in 2017 to expand its content palette and its primarily teen girl demographic in order to build its own convincing long-term monetization story. And, hey Americans, don't forget the rest of the world. Take China's mammoth WeChat and QZone, both owned by Tencent, as just two examples.

My focus here is on the major U.S.-based Media 2.0 players simply because my task would be endless otherwise. But, don't let that fool you. Behemoth social media networks compete overseas and push boundaries everywhere, increasingly with video.

And, remember we live in a borderless Media 2.0 world.

Chapter 10

● ● ●

DON'T FORGET ABOUT THE BRANDS!
(OR, "AND NOW A WORD ... I MEAN, VIDEO ... FROM OUR SPONSORS")

In these mobile and millennial-focused Media 2.0 times, it's not just the traditional media companies that finally understand that the world of content has radically changed. So do major brands. Gone are the days of the brand hammer. We have used our DVRs to skip those ads for years even on our big screens. The trick is to engage and entertain with new storytelling that works within different Media 2.0 realities, new platforms, new audiences, and the new sensibilities that go with them.

For brands, Media 2.0 means structural new marketing challenges. Yes, even the kids still find time to watch TV on the big screens in their living rooms. But, even in that last hallowed bastion of traditional media, they increasingly look down at their mobile phones. So, brands too must transform their thinking of what engagement looks like in this Media 2.0 world.

Branded content (also known as content marketing) gets most of the press. And, an effective branded content strategy certainly is a must in this day and age. Millennials almost expect branded messages now and accept them, so long as that content is entertaining, *authentically*. Digital-first media companies *(discussed earlier in Chapter 7)* offer the most obvious path to pursue those opportunities. Case in point, Whistle Sports' *Dude Perfect* boys use trickery to toss basketballs, instead of potato chips, into oversized Pringles cans *(that just made me hungry)*.

But, the boldest brands take things even further, transforming themselves into full-fledged media companies. No longer content simply making and marketing consumer packaged goods that touch consumers only intermittently, a few audacious brands look to establish an entirely different type of relationship and engage with their customers on an ongoing and deeply personal basis. They seek to associate themselves with a particular lifestyle category, and then become the voice and community for that category. These are what I call the new lifestyle media companies.

Red Bull continues to be THE prime example. The poster child. Red Bull is no longer just an energy drink, and hasn't been for a long time. It is now very much a media company focused on the lifestyles of aspiration and adrenaline *(which mean a broad swath of all of us, because who doesn't want to be a fearless adventurer?)*. Red Bull promotes that lifestyle – and, therefore, ultimately itself and its products – via brilliantly-executed premium video content like space parachuting Felix Baumgartner, a video that has been viewed by virtually everyone on this planet. Cans of caffeine are only one manifestation of that lifestyle and the primary way Red Bull monetizes. But not the only way.

To put an exclamation mark on this point, Red Bull established a completely separate major media operation in 2007 known as Red Bull Media House that operates much more than just Red Bull's marketing arm. It is measured by its own stand-alone financial success, and it actively courts outside clients. If you have any doubt about Red Bull's media strategy, check out the company's main website. Not one can of Red Bull in sight!

It's all about motorcycles, music festivals, and all kinds of cool places you'd rather be right now.

Other innovative major brands see Red Bull and this potentially game-changing Media 2.0 opportunity, and also hope to transform themselves into something much more than the products they sell. Marriott *(yes, that Marriott, the hotel chain)* boldly followed Red Bull's lead and launched its own major production studio in 2014, hoping to be the voice and home for millennial travel. Pepsi too has taken this route, building its own major studio in 2014 to produce digital-first content that speaks directly to a new generation of mobile-obsessed consumers who have grown tired of traditional marketing "speak."

In perhaps the most notorious Red Bull-inspired attempt, next-gen camera company GoPro positioned itself in 2014 to own the action-focused lifestyle media vertical, a seemingly logical story given the fact that GoPro-captured videos fill YouTube. GoPro effectively preached its media story to the Street and drove a massively successful IPO in the process. At one point, investors valued the company at a mouth-watering $8.1 billion. But, it now trades at a small fraction of that. Like Red Bull's Felix Baumgartner, GoPro's ambitions fell back to Earth with a massive thud in 2016 as the company ejected its media strategy and jettisoned most of its media team. I still scratch my head about that one.

Major brands, heed this call. As fast as you think you are moving now, move faster. Study Red Bull. Seek inspiration from Warner Bros.' brilliant 2017 marketing move with smash hit *Wonder Woman*. With the help of Intel, Warner Bros. literally brought motion picture marketing to new heights with the help of 300 perfectly synchronized drones in a dazzling, revolutionary light show. You can bet that social media accounts worldwide lit up the Internet, just as those drones lit up the evening sky.

Don't forget what Dollar Shave Club achieved with one single viral video. It's time to invest in Media 2.0. Significantly. Whether its bite-sized or super-sized, just get into the game. Right now.

Content, community, and commerce baby!

Chapter 11

● ● ●

THE MAINSTREAMING OF LIVE SOCIAL STREAMING

Internet-driven live video streaming certainly is nothing new. I served as CEO of SightSpeed 12+ years ago, and we offered both high quality one-to-one and one-to-many live video chat even back then – well before its mainstreaming via Skype video and Apple FaceTime. *(Logitech later acquired SightSpeed, because they saw the light – a very good deal for all, but did we sell too soon?)*. Several big fish, including YouTube and Major League Baseball via its BAMTech platform, have streamed major live events like the Olympics, Super Bowl and Coachella for several years now. Smaller fish too, like festival-focused live streaming pioneer BullDog Digital Media.

More traditional broadcast applications for live streaming are seemingly endless, of course – live sports, concerts, business events and conferences, as examples. That's why Disney invested $1 billion for a 33% share in BAMTech in 2016 – an investment that now will serve as the foundation for Disney's new SVOD ambitions. And, Turner bought a majority stake in competing live streaming company iStreamPlanet one year earlier.

One-to-many Internet-driven broadcast services like Twitch have catered to specific frequently non-obvious live-streaming use cases for quite some time, as well. In Twitch's case, the service live streamed gamer challenges and contests. So massive and valuable were Twitch and its audience, that Amazon scooped up the service in 2014 for nearly $1 billion *(see, there's that stealthy, crafty, somewhat insidious Amazon again)*. Could any of you reading this book have predicted that one?

Well, welcome to the mysterious, ever-changing and unexpected world of Media 2.0.

While live broadcast streaming is nothing new, live one-to-many "social streaming" at mass scale is. Our increasingly mobile-first world – and our increasingly robust networks to which they connect – take the live broadcast opportunity further downstream to each of us. We now can, and increasingly do, easily broadcast ourselves in high quality to our friends, our fans, the world via our mobile phones in a one-to-many way, rather than just in a FaceTime-ian one-to-one way. And, we promote these live streams through our social networks, which then play it forward (hence, the "social" in streaming).

What's particularly exciting here is that social streaming offers the potential to break down barriers between individual broadcasters – who are increasingly Media 2.0 personalities and "celebrities" of the kind discussed in Chapter 2 – and their audiences. Now true artist-fan engagement is possible, is happening, and holds the potential to be extremely lucrative, since fans are happy to directly support their favorite personalities.

Meerkat unleashed social streaming's possibilities en masse in 2015 and became an instant Media 2.0 darling. But, as is frequently the case in the world of Media 2.0, a much deeper-pocketed digital player – in this case Twitter – soon eclipsed Meerkat with its own "Periscope" app. Subsequently, in yet another case of survival-of-the-fittest where the strong prey on those beneath it in the food chain, Facebook stormed onto the social streaming scene with "Facebook Live" and dealt a significant blow to Twitter's pole position. Clever little Facebook even borrowed Twitter's magic number and signed 140 celebrities and companies to create live content at its launch. And, Facebook has no plans to follow Meerkat down its hole, throwing down a continuing string of new feature gauntlets in 2017 to hold onto the live streaming crown (including the addition of 360-degree live streaming).

Other live streaming-focused newbies include Live.ly, a 2017-born relative of mega-social app story Musical.ly that is yet another way for our kids to broadcast themselves to their friends in order to receive the validation they apparently so desperately crave (despite it being so obvious to us). Meanwhile, Former NBA Commissioner David Stern's new venture SportsCastr.Live enables all of us to be play-by-play announcers to our individual audiences.

As is always the case with any new technology, the fundamental question becomes how to effectively monetize it. Several ideas here in connection with live streaming.

First, social streaming is yet another powerful new Media 2.0 audience engagement and marketing tool. Brands can now launch products live and offer real-time incentives to attract us. Even more intriguingly, brands receive instant gratification feedback, as viewers react to events happening in real-time.

Second, traditional brand sponsorships offer obvious paths, as increasingly savvy marketers shift more dollars to new digital-first platforms like live streaming to generate more impact that is also more precisely measurable. Measurement, of course, means data. Facebook Live and the other major players collect reams of data about you as you merrily watch your favorite influencers. Just think of the value of that data to marketers. The main question becomes how fast and far will these services go to try to exploit it (and how much will we let them?).

Video-driven commerce also holds tantalizing possibilities, although those are more theoretical than real at this point. Social streaming also can be integrated into so-called "freemium" (free-to-pay) content strategies. Allow fans to watch the first few minutes of their favorite celebrity's streamed content for free, but then charge them to continue watching. Maybe even add a virtual tip jar to further support the cause, something that leading live streaming service "YouNow" enables. Or, perhaps offer the fleeting live stream for free, but then charge for later on-demand viewing of the archived version.

We are still very much in the early innings of live social streaming, but its reach into our daily lives and our overall collective consciousness just these past two years is impressive.

Chapter 12

● ● ●

TEN STRATEGIES FOR TODAY'S MEDIA 2.0 VIDEO WORLD

You now have a strong foundation in knowing what the key trends and who the lead actors are in the Media 2.0 world of video. Now, here is my list of 10 strategies that flow from those earlier chapters. Consider this your "cheat sheet" to kick off your own strategic discussions. Because specific examples are always useful, I identify concrete ways in which my business development and advisory firm CREATV Media can help (and already has helped) make these strategies become Media 2.0 realities – to give you actual, tangible and significant near-term "wins."

STRATEGY #1 – Content creators, know your distribution platform!
New platforms demand new stories and new ways to tell those stories. That's why, as we saw earlier, NBCUniversal and Time Warner now smartly develop entirely new content for Snapchat's new Shows service. That's why DirecTV Now features very different premium mobile-focused Originals than its millennial-focused Fullscreen child. And that's why traditionally formatted Warner Music Group music videos performed poorly on Snapchat's Discover at launch – standard traditional music videos simply didn't make the cut.

As a corollary, media companies can and should use Snapchat and other new Media 2.0 platforms as "farm clubs" – entry points to migrate and better monetize a significant number of digital natives who otherwise may never be exposed to traditional programming. Experiment efficiently with new digital-first characters and stories, and then take core elements from the most successful ones to develop related expanded stories for more traditional highly monetizable platforms. Remember Crypt TV? That's what I'm talking about. Highly visual, comics-driven multi-platform "motion book" start-up Madefire is another company worth watching in that regard. Even text can be powerful here. Check out Yarn, an LA-based startup that creates bite-sized, mobile-friendly episodic text narratives for our 2-minute "snackable" moments throughout the day.

My firm CREATV Media works with creators on both sides of the Media 2.0 divide to find new ways to tell new stories to a new kind of global audience and reach them via new multi-platform marketing strategies and partnerships. We connect the dots.

STRATEGY #2 – Even better, creators, take the core elements of your story on a continuing unified journey across all of Media 2.0's multiple platforms. Start small and social (mobile) – extend them into more traditional platforms (television, movies) – continue that journey of engagement into perhaps less obvious platforms (offline into the real world of live entertainment that I discuss later in Chapter 21, or even into brave new worlds like virtual and augmented reality which I discuss in Chapters 17 and 18) – and then bring the journey back home to its initial mobile, social roots.

Seize on a holistic overall approach to your storytelling. Now that's innovative! And that's also potentially both highly lucrative and transformational. Otter Media's Crunchyroll is a good example here as we have seen. Its management team views video content as being just the first step to build overall brand loyalty and "love" that it can then take to (and monetize on) other platforms, including live events and retail merchandise.

As I write this, my team and I are working with two companies doing just that – one, taking its leading digital-first video service into the real physical world, and the other, taking its very grounded (as in physical dirt) major music festival platform into the virtual online world of continuous content and community engagement in order to expand its customer relationships throughout the year, rather than during only one magical weekend.

STRATEGY #3 – Like Netflix, use data extensively to drive your content development and distribution strategies. That doesn't mean that you should use a soul-less "paint by numbers" approach to development of your Originals. No, that's not what Netflix does. Rather, Netflix, Amazon and others smartly use data to inform certain elements of their development decisions (what genres, who directs, who stars). You know, just like traditional media uses box office metrics. After all, philosophically at least, are those two approaches really that different? One is simply much more precise than the other.

The startup companies I mention above – Crypt TV, Madefire and Yarn – also use data to more efficiently target and find an audience receptive to stories and characters that are commercially deserving to be fleshed out further with more significant resources. In this way, the "green-lighting" process for expensive motion picture and television projects can add some real ROI-promising science to a traditional process that has been mired too much in pure subjectivity. That makes both right brains and left brains happy, because all business execs hope to drive greater financial and commercial success, while virtually all creators hope to drive greater artistic success and overall audience acceptance.

Bottom line – if you aren't extensively collecting and harnessing the full power of data right now and constantly investing in the latest Media 2.0

technology and services to do it, then you are leaving money on the table. Likely piles of it. Data represents more than a mere Media 2.0 opportunity. It's an outright necessity that can yield immediate ROI. My team and I work with companies to canvas the landscape of data collection and mining opportunities, identify leading innovators and "best practices," and secure ROI-transforming partnerships.

STRATEGY #4 – Although we still primarily watch our movies and television on traditional MVPD-delivered television, we increasingly rabidly watch Netflix and other OTT services. Now it's a question of how any one service differentiates itself and breaks through in this increasingly congested Media 2.0 world.

The uniform headline answer from all is to produce and distribute differentiated Originals and other exclusively-available content. Content, content, and then more content. That's why U.S. television featured over 500 original scripted series in 2016 alone – with 71 of those reported to be featured on or announced by Netflix. And, that's why many major premium OTT services now feature – or will soon feature – live MVPD-esque television channels in addition to VOD.

Use Originals smartly as a real differentiator. We work with both creators and distributors to match the best content with the best platform to achieve the best possible results.

STRATEGY #5 – **Another consistent strategy to breakout and win in the OTT video game is to focus on an underserved market segment that has no clear winner.** "Focus is your friend" in any business, and the OTT video world is no exception. Rather than try to be all things to all people like Netflix, Amazon or Hulu, target a specific passionate so-called "niche" audience (think of Crypt TV in the horror genre). If your content is compelling and your voice is authentic, those otherwise-neglected audiences may bite and spread the word. That's how most of the leading digital-first media companies discussed in Chapter 7 broke out.

Advertisers covet these more targeted demos and will pay more to reach them, particularly endemic brands that are already invested in relationships with these specific market segments. And, more targeted content holds the potential to monetize more effectively across the board, including via video-driven commerce. After all, underserved passionate niche audiences generally more actively seek out these more specialized, vertically-focused OTTs and are, therefore, more deeply engaged.

While many obvious content and lifestyle segments already count established leaders *(I discuss these in Chapter 7),* don't think for a minute that all have. We are a diverse people, after all. Now expand that globally. So-called "niche" audiences add up fast in a borderless world. You don't need to be everything to everybody in order to build a compelling, highly scalable and profitable media company that delights investors. That's why new players continuously rise up to lead where no one has staked a claim. Examples include "88 Rising" (pan-Asian content), "Crypt TV" (horror), and "Natcom Global" (multi-lingual health, wellness and news) – each of which I discussed earlier in Chapter 7.

My team and I regularly work with new digital-first media companies in unclaimed lifestyle segments. Action/outdoor, mid-tail amateur sports, and cannabis are just three that come to mind right now. Each very different. And, that's the point.

STRATEGY #6 – Active social engagement, sharing and community should be central elements of your video marketing, distribution and monetization strategies. Empower your audience to do the heavy lifting for you. Thrill them with your content, make it easy for them to share it, and offer ways to gather around it and communicate directly with both the creators and with each other. Don't forget to add the live social streaming element to make it even more personal and instantly actionable. Don't worry. You don't need to do this alone.

Companies frequently retain CREATV Media just for such purposes – to help chart their course of digital transformation via industry "best practices," as well as identify technologies and partners that can get them into the game quickly without significant expenditure of upfront capital or months and months of development.

STRATEGY #7 – Go global. Aggressively pursue international opportunities to significantly, yet efficiently, expand your marketing, distribution and monetization possibilities. After all, the Internet ties us all together in this borderless world. But, don't forget that successful international pursuit means recognition and respect for different and diverse cultures. That's why virtually all leading OTT services set up offices across the globe and seek out like-minded local partners. Global partners help navigate through the complexities of operating in a foreign land, and also add critical localized content that speaks uniquely to that particular culture and language.

HOOQ, mentioned earlier, is one example, bringing SingTel, Sony Pictures Entertainment and Warner Bros. together to beat back Netflix in Southeast Asia. And, Discovery Communications teamed up with European media giant ProSiebenSat.1 to conquer the German market. Netflix, on the other hand, failed to penetrate China on its own because it failed to establish close partnerships with Chinese companies that know how to navigate in that coveted territory's highly complex local systems. Two examples of two very different approaches and with two very different results.

CREATV Media works closely with companies and organizations both inside the U.S. and around the globe to bridge very different territories and cultures and find the right partnership "fit."

STRATEGY #8 – One-dimensional pure-play OTT video services must diversify their revenue streams. Yes, AVOD services like Vevo continue to proliferate in the OTT video space. But pressure mounts for these AVODs to add subscriptions and other perhaps not-as-obvious revenue streams like merchandising and live events to drive long-term profitability. That's why Hulu shut off its ad-only option in 2016 and introduced its virtual MVPD live television streaming service in 2017.

Pure-play SVOD services also must diversify to effectively compete with 800 pound gorillas Apple, Amazon, AT&T, Google, Verizon and others that drive multi-faceted business models. Amazon, with its ballooning multi-billion dollar Originals strategy, is about as multi-faceted as a Media 2.0 company gets *(much more on that in Chapter 21)*. That gives Amazon tremendous OTT freedom, including pricing and service bundling possibilities that others can't match.

The pure-plays can seek to diversify by building a deep library of proprietary Originals that they can incrementally monetize via lucrative licensing deals, a strategy that is now a major focus for both Netflix and Hulu. Or, instead, they can ultimately send up the white flag, stand up, move toward the exit nearest them, and leave the building with the best buyer. This second course of action will be the best long-term answer for most leading pure-play OTT services.

CREATV Media is regularly called into action to analyze the overall industry, identify the most compelling options, and then help clients choose the best path forward (including with whom to walk down that path).

STRATEGY #9 – Premium OTT video services like Netflix do, in fact, cannibalize traditional pay TV services. The related phenomena of cord-cutters and cord-nevers are very real. **Don't fight that Media 2.0 reality. Acknowledge it. Embrace it. Re-invent your story.** Make that reality a strength, not a threat.

Take Comcast for example. Comcast smartly hedges its bets. On the one hand, it smartly bundles Netflix in its X1 set top box platform and touts it as a major consumer benefit (essentially, all the content and related services you need in one place). At the same time, Comcast announced to the world in 2017 that it plans to launch its own SVOD service. And, Comcast also loudly markets multiple premium OTT video players heavily in connection with its broadband services, because we all are willing to pay for faster and faster pipes that carry our favorite programming.

And how about AT&T? AT&T paid up massively to buy Time Warner content in one of Media 2.0's most audacious deals. AT&T also already owns the data plans for a whole new generation of cord-nevers. Now, it will be able to feed those digital and social natives compelling premium content exclusively on its DirecTV Now service.

My team and I work with companies big and small to optimize their over-all positioning, map out strategic options amidst hyper-competition, and maximize their perceived enterprise value for strategic purposes. We first analyze their business to understand their strengths and weaknesses. Then, we help them understand the market in which they operate amidst Media 2.0 realities – and where that market is going. We next help them identify their optimal path forward, including their most effective positioning, in order to most effectively communicate who they are (their identity) and why their "story" (solutions and strategy) are uniquely compelling to both internal and external stakeholders.

By the end of this exercise – literally within weeks – the company's enterprise value in the eyes of external players shoots up by millions (even tens of millions) of dollars. And, that's by doing nothing more than engaging in this exercise! It's simply because the company better understands itself, the Media 2.0 world around it, and how best to package itself, prioritize and move forward in this brave new world.

This is not just theoretical. I have seen this immediately-transformational (and massively ROI positive) result time and time again. These clients later drove highly successful, massively shareholder-maximizing strategic outcomes for themselves – including both M&A and investment. And, we frequently helped them identify the best potential strategic partners to get there.

STRATEGY #10 – Brands and marketers, you too need to immerse yourselves in Media 2.0's transformational realities and aggressively pursue new ways to engage and beat back the competition. Branded content is the most obvious, but contemplate even more ambitious moves a la Red Bull.

My team and I help brands and marketers understand that the lines between their identities – and those of traditional media, entertainment and even technology companies – increasingly blur in a Media 2.0 world of content, community and commerce.

All are active participants in the Media 2.0 ecosystem. All are Media 2.0 companies.

Part II, Section 2

● ● ●

TODAY'S DIGITAL-FIRST MUSIC WORLD

Apple fundamentally changed the music game with iTunes and its $.99 digital downloads more than one decade ago. But, a funny thing happened in the past couple years. Digital downloads' dominance in the music industry – which, by definition, also meant Apple dominance – gave rise to a newly dominant OTT streaming model.

I anticipated this reality 15 years ago when I served as President & COO of Musicmatch, where we pioneered on demand streaming "back in the day" and were shockingly profitable doing it (Yahoo! ultimately acquired the company in 2004 for $160 million). I vividly recall virtually everyone in the music industry scoffing at the notion that consumers would ever leave their digital downloads behind for subscription streaming. Well, guess what, although it took a while, they did. The mass consumer market ultimately realized what we always believed – i.e., that "renting" and "owning" music makes no difference in a mobile-first, always-listening world with powerful wireless networks.

In fact, so-called "renting" songs via on-demand subscriptions gives you "More Taste" (Apple Music claims access to nearly 40 million songs) and is "Less Filling" (generally $9.99 per month for all those tracks instead of iTunes' $.99 per track rack rate or $20 for a single physical album). That's a truly amazing value proposition when you think about it, which gets even better for Amazon Prime customers who pay only $7.99 month for that unlimited music listening privilege.

Streaming revenues surpassed digital downloads for the first time in 2015, and now account for a rather astounding 62% of the U.S. music industry's overall $6.7 billion in revenues (according to the Recording Industry Association of America's ("RIAA") mid-year 2017 report). Paid subscriptions alone are up an eye-popping 61% year-over-year. 2016 marked the U.S. music industry's first period of double-digit growth in twenty years, and that double-digit growth extended into 2017. And, this transformational streaming trend is only expected to accelerate. Global music streaming revenues are expected to reach $9.1 billion in 2017 and, get this, Goldman Sachs expects them to more than triple and contribute $28 billion to a re-born $41 billion global music industry by 2030.

So, much-maligned streaming looks like it may become the industry's ultimate savior after all, also opening up other tantalizing revenue possibilities for artists in the process *(more on that in Chapter 15)*. And, to think that even Steve Jobs – the innovator amongst all innovators – once (in)famously said, *"The subscription model of buying music is bankrupt"* and couldn't be saved even by *"the Second Coming."*

Well, guess what's Coming in 1st place right now?

Chapter 13

● ● ●

THE RISE & DOMINANCE OF MUSIC STREAMING (& THE INDUSTRY'S YOUTUBE "PROBLEM")

Despite offering hope to Media 2.0 doubters in 2016 and 2017, the music industry's newly dominant streaming reality still doesn't make too many in the industry happy, with a few notable exceptions. In the minds of most media execs, as well as many highly respected artists, Apple iTunes economics were bad enough – stripping out singles from albums and selling them for, well, a song. A general refrain of devaluing content, denigrating artist integrity, and chilling overall artistic creativity filled the airwaves, especially in the early days of iTunes. But at least those downloads were easy to compartmentalize, track and pay.

Both ad-supported and subscription-based music streaming continue to be very different in most industry minds. Free ad-supported streaming radio services like Pandora classic – which give users no on-demand artist or song control – pay artists and labels a statutory per-stream royalty that represents a tiny fraction of a digital download royalty. On the other hand, paid subscription on-demand streaming services like Spotify – that give users full artist and song control – pay higher rates negotiated directly with the music labels that yield 6X the revenues of ad-supported streaming. Yet, even those higher rates yield pennies on the dollar in the minds of many traditionalists already feeling pummeled by downloads.

The stark reality is that virtually no one in the music industry – at least not yet – makes any real money on "just the music" anymore (with one notable exception … *wait for it*). Not the vast majority of artists. Not the labels. Not even Spotify and Pandora, the two leading pure-play streaming music services that arrived on the scene to challenge iTunes' download dominance. Neither has generated any ongoing profit. In fact, long-term profitability is still very much out of their reach *(more on that in Chapter 14)*.

So, artists and labels understandably demand more in terms of royalties, and the streaming services understandably beg to pay less, because nothing pencils out.

YouTube is the one glaring exception to the current pessimism that continues to surround the streaming music business model. And, in a reality that may surprise you, YouTube is the number one music listening platform – by far – for millennials.

Here's why. With the rise of smart phones, YouTube's video dominance also led to YouTube's music listening dominance, because the line that previously separated audio music experiences from pure music video experiences blurs in a mobile-first world. For millennials, it more like simply vanishes. Why pay for music when you can listen to it for free on YouTube? Video and the music within it are indistinguishable in an on-the-go smart phone environment. You simply don't watch it.

And, here's the punch line. Because of its video-first roots, YouTube's royalty structure is fundamentally different from all audio-first services. YouTube actually makes money on the music itself. Every time. It always wins (*"just like a casino*," in the words of one deeply knowledgeable label exec with whom I spoke, but preferred to remain nameless).

Yes, you read that right. YouTube's video roots give it a fundamental advantage over all pure-play streaming music services. And, while reports indicate that 40% of YouTube's videos are music-related, Apple's Jimmy Iovine laments that YouTube only accounts for about 4% of the music industry's overall revenues. The RIAA largely confirms "The Defiant One's" (Iovine's) analysis and published a 2017 report concluding that the current royalty system *"benefits platforms like YouTube and disadvantages companies like Spotify."*

You can only imagine how that makes others feel, and you'd be right – although let's not forget that the major music labels freely negotiated these deals with YouTube in the first place to create this state of affairs (and are now looking to "fix" them). Global music trade organization International Federation of the Phonographic Industry (IFPI) called YouTube the single greatest threat to the renewed growth of the music industry. And, Spotify used this un-level playing field to re-negotiate more favorable royalties from the major labels this past year, reportedly bringing down Universal Music Group's (the largest of the majors) royalty rates from 55% to 52%. Doesn't sound like much, but that 3% matters at Spotify's scale. A lot. Its gross margins reportedly improved from 15% to 22% in 2017.

That's why Vevo's sole major label holdout, Warner Music Group, finally agreed to directly license its videos to Vevo in 2016. Warner hopes to drive more viewing of its videos directly on Vevo (and away from YouTube) in order to reap significantly higher royalties. And, that's why it also entered into an innovative new distribution arrangement for its videos in 2017 with "under the radar" mobile-first video producer and distributor Natcom Global *(discussed earlier)*. Natcom gives Warner Music a major new platform that it can control and monetize more directly. Warner can incentivize and steer music lovers to watch its videos across Natcom's global channels by offering exclusive valuable content (like behind-the-scenes footage) that is not available anywhere else. In other words, off YouTube, rather than on it.

You can bet YouTube has a good explanation for its uniquely more favorable economics, and you'd be right there too. In a widely-circulated blog post mid-2016, YouTube's chief product officer Neil Mohan insisted that YouTube should be praised, rather than denigrated, because it has paid out over $3 billion to the music industry over time (including $1 billion in 2016 alone). Even more, he argued that YouTube single-handedly can be the music industry's savior. Mohan points the finger at terrestrial radio as being the real culprit behind today's continuing music industry angst. After all, good old-fashioned radio is quietly still perhaps the deepest music force in our daily lives, because we drive a lot. And, terrestrial radio also benefits from very different economics than its online brethren.

In a 2016 survey by research firm Cowen & Company, 74% of all respondents indicated that they listen to terrestrial radio significantly more than second place YouTube's 59% (although Cowen concludes that *"YouTube is the leading source of music for millennials"*). A surprising 93% of millennials even listen to AM/FM radio according to Nielsen. And, terrestrial radio pays absolutely nothing directly to artists and labels and, instead, keeps virtually all advertising revenues for itself. Mohan contends that the music industry's size would double *(yes, 2X!)* if just twenty percent of radio and television advertising revenue shifted online *(which, surprise surprise, certainly wouldn't hurt Google's advertising-driven bottom line either)*.

YouTube's head of music, long-time music industry mogul Lyor Cohen, double-downed on Mohan's 2016 blog post with his own high profile article in August 2017. In it, Cohen argued first that YouTube actually pays higher royalty rates than other ad-supported free streaming services. Second, he proclaimed to the industry that YouTube should be applauded for creating more breakout artists than any other service (who then achieve visibility and monetize in myriad ways not traceable back to YouTube).

Not so fast, retorted the RIAA's CEO Cary Sherman, who immediately responded with a fiery post that asks, *"Why is YouTube paying so little?"*

In it, Sherman writes that YouTube pays music creators far less than 400 other digital music services on both a per-stream and per-user basis. And, Richard James Burgess, CEO of the American Association of Independent Music, piled on with language mirroring debates about 2017's Charlottesville tragedy (one of many tragedies in a seemingly particularly cataclysmic year). Writing *"there is absolutely no moral equivalency between Spotify and YouTube,"* Burgess flat out rejected Cohen's assertions, countering that *"Spotify commits to pay creators with every play of their music,"* while YouTube *"chooses when they will pay, what they will pay, and the circumstances under which they will pay."*

In other words, most in the industry still don't buy YouTube's position.

Perhaps it's because the last tech titan(ic) music force in the industry also came from Silicon Valley and cloaked itself as being a "savior" *(although that one dressed in a black turtleneck bought in Cupertino).*

You can bet the music industry remembers.

Chapter 14

● ● ●

MUSIC'S STREAMING WARS
(CAN ANY PURE-PLAY WIN AGAINST THE BEHEMOTHS?)

YouTube, Spotify, Pandora, Apple Music, Amazon Music Unlimited, Tidal, SoundCloud – these are the main cast of characters in the global music streaming wars that now dominate the music industry. New players continuously enter the market, and many old ones leave. Amazon Music Unlimited launched in October 2016 to disrupt the entire streaming game and its long-established $9.99 monthly subscription price point, while Samsung quietly and downright sheepishly closed the door on its essentially-overlooked Milk Music service in 2016.

Market realities nearly pulled the plug on music darling SoundCloud in 2017. Even with its significant global reach and monetization (the company says its annual revenue run rate reached $100 million as of August), SoundCloud still bleeds cash. Late summer, as zero hour approached (always a good time for white knights to extract the best deal terms), media-focused private equity firm Raine Group and Singapore's sovereign wealth fund Temasek injected $169.5 million into the company to keep the wheels on the bus and now own most of it.

Others like iHeartRadio, Deezer, and the second coming of Napster *(okay, maybe third, since this version is re-branded Rhapsody)* continue to languish in folksy solitude, generating little attention at all. Meanwhile, near year-end 2017, little-known media company LiveXLive signed a deal to acquire near-forgotten Slacker for a surprisingly robust $50 million, contingent upon a successful IPO.

Let's take a look at where things stand right now with the key players in this Media 2.0 music space in which YouTube *(as discussed in Chapter 13)* is the dominant force for millennials.

I. SPOTIFY & PANDORA – THE LEADING PURE-PLAYS

Spotify is the closest thing to holding Netflix-ian dominance amongst music streaming services. You and I both probably use it. As of Q3 2017, Spotify counts 60 million paying subscribers (of its total 150+ million audience) for its $9.99 monthly on-demand streaming service across 60+ countries. That's up from 40 million paying subs in Q4 2016. Spotify also offers ad-supported radio-like free streaming.

We also likely listen to Pandora. Prior to 2017, Pandora offered only less-controlled radio-like streaming in two flavors – free ad-supported, or ad-free at $4.99 monthly. But, in a major strategic shift to significantly improve its overall challenged economics, Pandora launched its own "Spotify-Killer" on-demand service in 2017 at a now-familiar $9.99 monthly price point. Pandora announced big plans when it did, forecasting 6-9 million paying subscribers by end of 2017.

But, those lofty goals hit cold stark reality soon thereafter when the company reported only 390,000 paying subscribers to its new service as of Q2 2017. Even worse, it reported that its active listener count had actually declined. And, as year-end 2017 approached, while Pandora's active user base approached 80 million monthly users (an impressive number to be sure), roughly only 5% of were paying customers – and the vast majority of those pay for Pandora classic at $4.99 monthly rather than the higher-priced Spotify-like service. That's why interim CEO Naveen Chopra advised the industry in Q3 2017 that Pandora would re-focus its efforts on its free user base, *not relying on the subscription model as much as in the past.*

Spotify and Pandora (and Tidal, Napster, Deezer, and Slacker) are pure-plays like Netflix and Hulu on the video side, which almost exclusively monetize just the music itself via ads, subscriptions, or both. As a result, most continue to bleed cash. Spotify alone is reported to have lost more than $600 million in 2016, and was on a similar path for 2017 despite gargantuan revenues expected to reach $5 billion. And we already know why. These pure-play music services face the same challenge – the same existential crisis – that Netflix and Hulu confront on the video side against multi-faceted behemoths Apple, Amazon, AT&T and YouTube. As discussed in Chapter 4, the business models of those tech behemoths differ fundamentally from those of stand-alone pure-play OTT streaming services. For Apple, Amazon and YouTube, content (in this case music) is simply a means to an end. Not the end itself.

That's why Pandora, like SoundCloud, needed a life-line in 2017. And it got one in June in the form of a $480 million investment from SiriusXM, which acquired a 19% stake in the company in the process. Will SiriusXM ultimately convert its 19% "try" to a full 100% "buy" via M&A?

Certainly wouldn't surprise me, because neither Spotify nor Pandora can stand alone long-term as independents unless they achieve some kind of new monetization breakthrough. They will instead end up playing strategic roles in a much bigger machine. In the belly of one of the behemoths.

II. THE BEHEMOTHS

Speaking of … now it's time for the giants that have the luxury of being able to use music as marketing.

APPLE

Let's first take Apple. Apple Music is one big advertisement for Apple hardware (iPhones, Macs). Content is its Trojan Horse. Apple Music succeeds even if Apple Music doesn't generate $1 of profit. But, that doesn't mean that Apple Music isn't strategic for Apple, because it most certainly is. Apple needed an on-demand music streaming service to counter its declining iTunes music download business and continue to drive the faithful into its kingdom of hardware delights. Unable to build it itself, Apple looked into the marketplace and found a kindred spirit in streaming service Beats (a company that shared Apple's DNA by operating primarily in the hardware business with its headphones).

Apple Music offers two tiers of music streaming – monthly $9.99 or $14.99 for a family plan *(note to self – Apple also quietly offers a $99 annual plan that can be unearthed with some digging)*. As of June 2017, Apple Music boasted over 27 million paying subscribers, more than double its numbers from one year earlier. Impressive – a feat driven by Apple's unique ability to bundle and headline Apple Music across all of its Apple products.

That's certainly a luxury that no pure-play has.

AMAZON

Amazon's multi-pronged business model is like Apple's, but also very different. Yes, Amazon too sells hardware, including the surprisingly massively successful Kindle and Alexa-driven Echo. But, unlike Apple, Amazon is not and never will be fundamentally a hardware business. Amazon is all about commerce pure and simple. Selling stuff. And lots of it. So, Amazon's Music Unlimited subscription service, as well as its companion Amazon Prime Video service, function as Apple-like gateways to Amazon's virtual mega-mall and its increasing focus on mobile shopping. Like Apple, Amazon doesn't need to profit from the music itself, and that gives it great business and competitive freedom.

Amazon flexed those threatening muscles big time when it launched Amazon Music Unlimited late 2016 with a disruptive new monthly price point $2 lower than the competition ($7.99 for Amazon Prime customers). Amazon's royalty rates with the major music labels likely aren't any different than those of the pure-plays, but Amazon simply can "eat" that extra $2 and spread it across its overall financials.

Scary indeed for those that can't.

GOOGLE/YOUTUBE

Ahh yes, and then there's the biggest 800 pound Media 2.0 music gorilla of them all, YouTube – a very different animal altogether *(as I discussed at length in Chapter 13)*. We now already know that YouTube continues to feel virtually uniform industry wrath for its very different economics that flow from its very different video-first DNA. Yet, YouTube nonetheless succeeded in negotiating new licensing deals with all major labels in 2017, because its strategic position in the overall music industry is now simply too cemented in millennial lives.

As 2017 began, Google also operated its Google Play Music and YouTube Red streaming services (the latter at the usual $9.99 monthly price). But, both services pale in significance to music on YouTube itself and, as the year progressed, YouTube announced plans to merge those confusing services that together count 7 million subscribers as of August. After all, both services (whether separate or unified) are all about driving Google's fundamental underlying and seemingly unlimited advertising-based cash machine – just keeping its overall user base entertained amidst increasingly predatory competition.

That's quite a differentiator and competitive advantage.

III. THE WRATH OF THE TITANS

Apple, Amazon and Google/YouTube also control massive marketing dollars outside the wildest dreams of the pure-plays. Apple continuously bombards us with Apple Music pitches in its own characteristic "sexy" way, with every breath you take and every move you make, across all of its platforms – both virtual (online) and physical (offline retail stores). There is no escape. And, to be absolutely sure, Apple features Apple Music natively on all Apple devices (iPhone, Macbooks). No app install is needed. That's immediate distribution – and headlining – that Spotify and the others can't match.

The behemoths also certainly have the ability to invest significantly more deeply in artist relations and artist exclusives – differentiated content that is increasingly critical for these services in this aural battle royale (just like the strategic role Originals play in the Media 2.0 video world). Steve Jobs played to artist sensibilities from day 1, and Apple underscored the strategic nature of its heritage when it retained Jimmy Iovine and Dr. Dre as part of its Beats acquisition. Meanwhile YouTube, faced with mounting music industry pressure, smartly hired long-time music executive Lyor Cohen as its new head of music in order to try to quell the music industry masses about YouTube's advantageous economics. We saw in Chapter 13 how well that has gone so far.

Spotify, on the other hand, seemingly bit the hand that feeds over the years and counted a very vocal and very bitter Taylor Swift and Radiohead – in addition to the labels themselves – as foes at various points. Sweden's Spotify – born a long, long way from the U.S.-based music industry – proudly celebrated its colder tech-based roots first and foremost in its early days, ignoring the music industry's more sunny soulful essence until it learned the hard way. The company finally atoned when it hired well-known, highly respected entrepreneur and artist manager Troy Carter (Lady Gaga, John Legend, among others) as its new global head of creator services in 2016. These kinds of gestures matter.

Spotify hopes to flex some muscle of its own when it finally goes public. But, regardless of its eventual purse when it does, Spotify and the other pure-plays will continue to face daunting challenges in the face of giants. Yet, in the immortal words of Yoda (as he fixes his gaze upon Spotify, Pandora and the others, based on his own intergalactic challenges), *"Do, or do not. There is no try."* So, "do" they do.

Here's how. First, Spotify will catch the Tidal wave *(clever, huh?)* and increasingly feature artist and song exclusives like it did this year when it dropped Jay Z's latest first. Content is king here in the music world too – the most critical differentiator – and featuring Jay Z is massively more important to boosting paid subscriber numbers than adding yet another service feature. The trick, of course, is for the pure-plays to find a way to continuously incentivize artists and labels to work with them rather than with the deeper-pocketed big guys. Tidal got the job done by making Jay Z and a few other marquee artists part owners. So, that's one option. Spotify, of course (much like Snapchat versus Instagram), also will continue to try to out-innovate on the feature and user experience side of the house. Its "Discover Weekly" personalized playlists were a big taste-making hit in 2017.

Even more fundamentally – nay, critically – Spotify and other pure-play music services will try to diversify their one-dimensional business models. Yes, everyone around the world uses Spotify, but that doesn't mean that stand-alone music streaming businesses are long-term sustainable. Conversion rates from free ad-supported music streaming to ad-free paid subscription streaming are simply too low. Even if they weren't, today's licensing realities and overall economics just don't pencil out. That's why mid-2017, Spotify announced re-positioning its overall advertising opportunity. Now, Spotify plans to build a leading ad sales business targeting small and medium businesses and with the audacious goal of becoming the world's third biggest digital advertiser next to Google and Facebook. So, look forward to seeing more and more sponsored playlists and new audio ad formats.

At around the same time, Spotify also announced that it would begin to focus on podcasts, a throwback format that continues to be shockingly popular. Bloomberg reports that about 15% of U.S. individuals over age 12 listen to at least one podcast weekly – and nearly 25% of us at least one monthly. Even better, podcast ad revenues are forecast to close up 85% in 2017. That's some massive growth. Importantly, podcasts don't come with music's massive licensing price tag. Those royalties accounted for an EBITDA-killing 75% of Spotify's costs in 2016. And, in another new strategic area of focus, Spotify also now integrates with Google's Home smart speaker in its quest to enhance its monetization hopes and dreams.

As discussed at length in Chapter 6, one of Spotify's previous big bets to change the order of things is our good old friend video Originals, although by year-end 2017 its video ambitions had significantly narrowed to be playlist-focused. But, Spotify still hopes that seeing is believing in a pay-worthy and broader music lifestyle experience kind of way. Tidal succeeded briefly in that regard when it debuted Beyonce's incredible long-form *Lemonade* video in 2016 and boosted its paid subscription numbers significantly in the process.

Pandora itself announced major video plans in 2016, but we didn't see much happen there in 2017. In any event, video game playing by pure-plays Spotify and Pandora won't be easy. Their DNA is music, and we go to both Spotify and Pandora to listen. It's not obvious that we will think of those services more broadly. Pattern behavior, after all. And, of course, the OTT premium video market is increasingly downright saturated. Maybe that's precisely why both Spotify and Pandora, which trumpeted their video scores loudly as 2017 began, decrescendo-ed those notes throughout the year.

Pandora previously had placed its own major diversification bet in 2015 when it bought ticketing agency Ticketfly for $335 million, thereby adding an entirely new (and seemingly logical) revenue stream. But, schizophrenically, it changed course and sold off that tantalizing new piece to Eventbrite in 2017 for a jaw-dropping $135+ million less than it paid just two years earlier. So, whereas Pandora once sang loudly and proudly to the world that Ticketfly would broaden its overall appeal to become the single home for the music lifestyle (not just the home for the music itself), it lowered its multi-platform voice to a whisper-like *sotto voce* in 2017 and returned to its rather one-dimensional refrain in the name of focus. All I can say is, "Wow!" *(as in, sigh, non-caps "wow").*

So what else can the pure-plays do to surmount their daunting challenges in the face of seemingly impenetrable behemoths?

Why not take their broader revenue-generating quest significantly further by engaging much more directly with their users who are massive and frequently rabid artist fans? Fan engagement means live events, compelling e-commerce (merchandise), and direct artist-fan and community engagement. Hey Spotify and Pandora! Focus on deeply integrating those components into your overall customer experiences and, man, significant monetization (not to mention brand love and loyalty) will follow. No music streaming service does that right – no, not even the behemoths. Music is unlike any other form of media in terms of its impact on our lives. Artists are our messiahs. Tap into that transformational human element – that's where the magic happens *(more on this in Chapter 15)*. Fans will pay (a lot!) for that direct connection, as well as for a direct link to others in the community who feel the same way about the artist as they do.

Even so, the pure-play existential crisis is unlikely to resolve itself in the face of behemoth super-powers, which means that Spotify's and Pandora's most likely end games are to be swallowed up in true Apple/Beats-ian fashion. Like the big banks, Pandora and Spotify are simply too big to fail, of course. One of the many Goliaths out there will bail them out instead. After all, many have the means necessary, as we saw when AT&T dropped $85 billion to buy Time Warner. Yes, pure-play stand-alone economics may not work, but their respective brands, global audience reach and overall engagement in our daily lives do.

How many of us listen to streaming music services for hours each day? (*I know I do, virtually 24/7 – it keeps me sane as I continuously edit this book*). That's some kind of reach. And, Goliath buyers can amortize the singular, fundamentally challenged pure-play business models across all of their many revenue streams. After all, they can simply throw those challenged financials into their marketing expense lines. So, in the immortal lyrics of one of my favorite 80's bands *Tears For Fears*, these Media 2.0 music realities inevitably will be *"sowing the seeds"* of M&A for Spotify, Pandora, and a host of others. They did for Slacker in 2017.

Of course, that means fewer competitors in the music distribution game – certainly not the optimal reality for any supplier (in this case the music labels). The more competition, the better. More demand for the content that fuels that competition. More leverage in negotiations. More lucrative terms. Feels almost like those "big box" days of yore, when Walmart and Target used music as loss-leaders to drive sales of paper towels. Don't forget, Amazon is kind of doing that now by charging $2 less per month for Amazon Music Unlimited for its Prime customers so that they stay in their virtual store and buy more, well, paper towels (and all kinds of other stuff that most certainly is not music). That race-to-the-bottom pricing pressure and overall mentality ultimately killed the pure-play Tower Records and Virgin Megastores of the past.

Quite a different state of affairs, then, from what's happening in Media 2.0's video side of the house. While the number of streaming music players continues to shrink, it's "go, go, go" time in the world of streaming video, where we see a continuing string of new market entrants joining the long list of OTT players already in the game – all kicking and screaming to create and license as much premium video content as possible (and significantly driving up video content prices in the process).

Music and video. Both premium content. But, very different rules of the game, because of the very different players who wrote them.

Which streaming music services will independently stand at the end of 2018?

Text me your predictions now.

Chapter 15

● ● ●

A SPECIAL WORD TO MUSIC ARTISTS ("DON'T FEAR THE STREAMING REAPER")

Musicians, how can you actually make money (monetize) in this brave, yet sometimes frightening, new digital world that has completely disrupted (more like shattered) longtime business models? We already know from Chapter 13 that streaming music services like YouTube, Spotify and Pandora drive significantly less direct revenues to artists themselves, at least at this point. Right?

Yes, that's certainly true if streaming service revenues are considered in isolation. But, for the vast majority of musicians – all except the biggest names – it's not primarily about selling the music itself. Was that ever enough to support your calling anyhow? Instead, it's about touring. It's about getting out to your old fans and making new ones by connecting and engaging directly with them. And, that's something that this brave new online world enables in a way that was never before possible. A new kind of direct-to-audience linkage is available to all musicians – established or not – anytime, anywhere, 24/7. The Internet has democratized overall opportunities available to musicians and significantly expanded opportunities for discovery, engagement and obsessive listening.

Streaming's potential, then, is to expand artist revenues by opening the door to new fans and deepening direct fan-artist engagement – and all of the myriad tantalizing new revenue opportunities that go with it. I call this a new "community-based" business model for artists in which each individual revenue stream today may be significantly less than streams of the past, but taken together, they ultimately hold the potential to drive greater overall revenues.

In this new community-based business model, the goal of artists should be to open as many legitimate doors as possible for fans to experience their songs. Yes, many fans may be reluctant to pay for content that they have been sadly conditioned to believe is "free." But, they are more than happy to fork over big cash to get closer to you, the artists and bands they love. Sprinkle in direct access for your fans to your daily life *(your hopes, your dreams, your shows, your world – yourselves!)* and you really begin to build something. "Things" you can monetize. Music fans will pay for that kind of access. Fan clubs have proven that. Fans also will pay extra (frequently significantly extra) for "experiences" that expand your live show's impact.

Here's one example. In 2015, oft-overlooked long-time streaming service Rhapsody (now resurrected in the guise of Napster 3.0) implemented a significant strategic partnership with artist-fan engagement service BandPage to bring unique offers like VIP meet-and-greets into their overall streaming experiences. So, let's say you stream Beyonce. Now, you receive notifications for her upcoming shows, as well as potentially other "goodies." Here's another. Inspiring startup Seeds gives artists an ability to connect with your fans directly to follow your ongoing creative journeys – including every person, place and sound featured in each song on your next album. Think of it as a microscope's view into your and your song's DNA. And your fans may even have a chance to influence it. How cool is that?

It's up to artists, their representatives, and the services themselves to explore all tantalizing possibilities. To experiment. Seed's new direct fan engagement paradigm – and Napster's treasure trove of data with BandPage's artist tool-set – give hope to new transformational possibilities. So does LA-based Repost Network, a music startup that identifies "under the radar" trending SoundCloud artists and adds their own kind of rocket fuel to get them noticed (and monetized). And, let's not forget that streaming revenues themselves continue to surge.

Musicians, listen up. Be entrepreneurial. Put yourselves out there. Use all available means to establish direct connections with your fans. Grant them access. Create unique experiences. Most importantly, experiment in this brave new Media 2.0 world. Throw caution to the wind and test the ever-increasing set of new artist-friendly programs offered by leading music streaming services that need you more and more each day as a result of feverish competition. Remember, those services can't be kings in this streaming game without you and your songs.

Your experiments today may lead you to the promised land of actually being able to afford your music career. Perhaps even thrive.

Imagine that.

Chapter 16

●　●　●

CREATORS – ISSUES TO CONSIDER WHEN USING MUSIC IN VIDEO & MORE
(by Jordan Bromley, Partner, Manatt Phelps & Phillips)

So, you want to add music to your videos, games, immersive experiences or other works? How do you properly "clear" it? Many don't understand that there is no "safe harbor" for use of music in a video or any other work. No matter how short, no matter how limited the views, no matter how you credit the creators, if you use music and you don't clear it, you are an infringer. Bottom line – this is something you must do.

Here are some tips to do things right.

(1) There are two "sides" to every song – the musical composition and the master recording. Think of the composition as the sheet music, the song that you sing. Think of the master as the recording of that song. The composition is eternal, and the master is the recorded moment where you perform that eternal work. You must "clear" both.

(2) The relevant clearance is called a "synchronization license" ("synch license" for short) since you are synchronizing the audio to the video. Boiled down, you need a synchronization license from both the composition owner(s) and the master owner(s), each of which can be several people if more than one collaborated in writing the composition or own the master. Generally speaking, however, there is normally one person or entity that owns or controls the master. And, you must get these before you share your video, game, immersive experience, or any other audiovisual work with the world. It doesn't matter if you're making money or not, and it doesn't matter how little of the composition and master you use. If you use any recognizable part of the composition or master recording, don't take the risk. Clear it.

If a song is popular, you can bet that companies control each "side." Music publishers control the musical composition, and record labels generally control the master recording. Not to belabor the issue, but even if the writer or recording artist says they are okay with your use, you still need an official clearance from each of the relevant company stakeholders. Seasoned clearance companies first issue a quote for any proposed use, and then require longer form license agreements once there is actual use.

In an interesting related side-note, Facebook faced a significant dilemma when it launched its new "Watch" video service in summer 2017. Watch included a massive number of UGC videos that incorporated music without the necessary clearances. Because Facebook had not yet developed a YouTube-like Content ID-like system, Facebook was reported to have offered the major record labels "hundreds of millions of dollars" so that they wouldn't need to take-down those infringing videos – and to enable Facebook users to upload their frequently music-infringing UGC content on a going-forward basis.

(3) Become familiar with the concept of "Most Favored Nations" (or "MFN" for short). MFN clauses in license agreements are a way for the various music owners to make sure no owner is earning more on the license than any other owner. They are also a way to legally "game" the clearance system. If you can find one sympathetic owner to grant a less expensive or "gratis" license, you can then try to use that friendly agreement to get all other owners to play nice on an MFN basis with the first licensor. As you can imagine, this requires great finesse and knowledge of the major publishers and labels that own a majority of the world's musical content.

(4) You don't need a license from every co-owner of the composition or master. A more complicated way exists to get around a stubborn songwriter, publisher or record label in the rare instances that involve co-owned masters. Put simply, under the real property concept of joint tenancy, one owner can grant a non-exclusive license for 100 percent of the work, provided that the other owners are paid their respective portion of the income made from the license. Of course, the co-owner needs to know of, and approve, the fact that they are clearing 100 percent of the work.

But, note that this is a particularly hot-button issue with songwriters right now. Without getting too granular, the largest performance rights organizations in the U.S. *(more on these below)* are fighting with the U.S. Department of Justice over whether they must issue 100 percent licenses, rather than the previous standard of licensing only individual shares. Long story short, if you attempt to use the strategy discussed above, you may run into more roadblocks at this point based on the current state of affairs.

(5) Don't forget about public performance licenses!

If you're exhibiting your music-laden video or other work on your own website, you need to obtain a public performance license in addition to the synch license. This separate license gives you the right to play the music in a public venue (which, in this case, is your public-facing website). Public performance licenses are generally issued by performance rights organizations ("PROs"). ASCAP and BMI are the two largest PROs and are bound by a consent decree with the Department of Justice, which means they must grant you this type of license if you request it – even if you disagree on the relevant fee.

What happens if you never agree on a fee? The dispute then goes to what is called "rate court" and a judge decides for you. Note that this comes with significant legal costs.

(6) Consult an Expert. If you're serious about your project, it makes sense to spend a little money to talk to an expert in this field. There are many clearance companies who can help you clear music in your video, game, immersive project or other work for reasonable flat fees. Look into it and hire one. At the very least, it will save you countless hours of figuring out who to contact and what to say.

Music rights are incredibly complex and messy. You don't want to run into costly legal issues – or, even worse, an order to "cease and desist" – once your video or other creation starts to gain traction.

Do the right thing now.

Part II, Section 3

●　●　●

OUR IMMERSIVE NEW MEDIA 2.0 WORLD OF VR, AR & MR

Video in our Media 2.0 world. Check. Music. Check. Now it's time to explore Media 2.0's related immersive technologies – virtual reality (VR), augmented reality (AR), and so-called mixed reality (MR).

2016 marked the year when both VR and AR broke out into the Media 2.0 mainstream. VR, as expected. AR, not so much *(okay, not at all – it took the long overlooked and somewhat mocked world of Pokemon to make that happen)*. 2017, on the other hand, represented a quieter and gentler overall immersion of these newly-commercialized technologies into our collective consciousness and daily lives. Research firm IDC forecast the combined VR/AR market to finish 2017 at $13.9 billion, an increase of 130.5% over the $6.1 billion spent in 2016. And, IDC pegs the combined immersive market opportunity to reach $143.3 billion by 2020. Meanwhile Goldman Sachs predicts sales of VR and AR headsets alone to reach over $95 billion and overtake TV sales by 2025.

AR is ultimately expected to dwarf the overall VR market by about 4 to 1. Analyst firm Digi-Capital projects over one billion AR users and $83 billion in mobile AR revenues alone by 2021. It's easy to see why. We can go about our daily lives and actively engage with others in an AR world, because AR overlays digital content and data on a real world that we fully see. We can't do that in a fully-immersed, completely virtual and more solitary VR world, where you are literally blind to everything not in your headset.

MR differs slightly from AR by layering synthetic, virtual content over our actual realities, sometimes even without a headset or handheld device. Disney wowed the world in 2017 with its *Magic Bench* "walk-up-and-play" MR experiment that enabled multiple users to *feel* the presence of CGI characters and interact with them.

Another fascinating and related immersive storytelling concept is "volumetric filmmaking" – think holographic characters that you, the moviegoers, can view from any angle at any moment in time. How will that work? Who knows, but many are trying, including Paramount's new Futurist Ted Schilowitz *(yes, that's his title)*, who also doubles as co-founder of HypeVR, a company that offers technology to give us all what they call "six degrees of freedom" with our media experiences. LA-based VNTANA takes things even further. In fall 2017, this pioneer announced the first-ever artificial intelligence hologram, enabling us to interact with "live" *(well, kind of)* person(alities) in physical real-world settings (theme parks, sporting events, retail, etc.).

The media and entertainment world is fascinated by these immersive technologies, as it should be. VR, AR and MR hold tremendous promise to expand the connection to, and impact of, content over time. And, the sheer numbers involved are staggering. Just think of all the content needed to fuel the coming onslaught of immersive technology and experiences.

Notice a recurring theme here creators? You should. Yes, that's right. Content is king, and the new immersive world of Media 2.0 not only craves it, it needs it in order to fulfill its massive potential and seize its overall transformational market opportunity.

Chapter 17

● ● ●

VR – THE VIRTUAL GETS VERY REAL

A Hollywood meeting doesn't seem to go by without some discussion of VR and its possibilities, and VR headsets now litter entertainment company conference rooms across Burbank. That's smart *(so long as those headsets really are used and aren't seen as being mere novelties ... because they aren't)*. But virtually all with whom I discuss VR still think too small, move too slowly, and treat VR like it is merely a separate and distinct product category or just another distribution platform.

Only that isn't the reality. In the minds of many, like Paramount's Futurist Ted Schilowitz who previously future-ized at Fox, VR is nothing less than game-changing. Geek standout publication *WIRED* effusively agrees, pronouncing VR as *"creating the next evolution of the Internet – an Internet of experiences."* Chew on that for a bit, and understand that you likely can't even comprehend how impactful VR can be until you have had your first premium VR experience – because, yes, it's true, you never forget your first time.

Samsung, HTC, Oculus and a host of others sold millions of premium consumer headsets in 2017. Millions more Google Cardboard and other more rudimentary smart phone-based VR headsets served as "gateway drugs" to those higher quality (and significantly more expensive) experiences, giving consumers a taste of VR so that they crave more.

VR's most obvious "here and now" promise is in the world of games, a market that few doubt will be massive. But VR-targeted animation and live action entertainment are expected to follow in short order. And smart, forward-thinking media and entertainment companies already are actively experimenting and placing their bets.

Fox has been amongst the most aggressive to date. After its well-received VR foray *The Martian VR Experience* in 2016, Fox immersed itself completely in 2017 by launching an entirely new VR unit called FoxNet and partnering with the likes of VR innovator Chris Milk and his company Within *(discussed below)* to produce *Planet of the Apes* experiences, among others. Sony also has been relatively aggressive in VR. Late 2016, Sony Pictures announced a partnership with Nokia *"to explore the creative potential"* of VR production and distribution. And, in June 2017, Sony announced a new *Breaking Bad* VR project with that iconic show's creator, Vince Gilligan. Imagine what it will feel like to "break bad" spherically? Who needs *Breaking Bad's* drugs when you are fully immersed in 360 degrees? That actually may freak you out more than the drugs!

And then there's Sky in the UK. After opening its own VR production studio in 2016, this U.K. media force announced plans for twelve new VR film projects in 2017. Meanwhile, Verizon's AOL (via its RYOT subsidiary) created a new team focused on VR and AR to bring immersive stories to life for major legacy brands that include *Sports Illustrated*.

Even the venerable Gray Lady, *The New York Times* – amongst the oldest of old media – got fired up about the possibilities *(cue the "Applause" sign)*. Beginning in late 2015, she distributed over one million Google Cardboards to her subscribers, seeing VR as being a critical new way to expand journalistic impact and extend her overall life expectancy amidst digital's relentless attack on print. The Lady extended those initial experiments this year when she developed a "VR companion piece" to George Saunder's novel, *Lincoln in the Bravo*. Marketers also jumped on board, spending real ad dollars and developing innovative brand-centered immersive experiences. In one notable example, outdoor apparel company Merrell used VR to launch a new hiking book, creating the buzz-worthy VR experience *Trailscape* that guided customers on a dangerous mountain hike.

So, now it's content's turn. If Media 2.0 builds it, more and more consumers most certainly will come. VR represents a once-in-a-generation rare opportunity to build an entirely new transformative media and entertainment kingdom. But how? How do creators solve VR's trickiest dilemma of transforming headset-laden solitary experiences into more social shared experiences? Even more fundamentally, how do creators even develop and produce live action VR stories? Imagine trying to direct a fully-immersive live action VR experience, choreographing all actions at once in a 360 degree spherical setting. How do you even begin to direct your talent, or focus an audience on one particular element in those spherical conditions? That's what VR innovator Chris Milk and others are trying to invent.

Storytellers must first develop an entirely new language of "experience," a new lexicon for VR, if you will, to address these foundational mind-bending challenges. Consider these to be VR entertainment's early days, much like the early days of cinema a century before. Just as today's movies evolved from those early rudimentary experiments, today's actions by bold Media 2.0 players ultimately will lead us to a new immersive promised land. We just don't know what those experiences will look ... er ... *feel* like. And that's part of the fun – simply imagining the possibilities.

Immersed in this background, here are some key players in the burgeoning Media 2.0 world of live action VR. I intentionally exclude leading headset-focused consumer electronics companies like HTC, Samsung, and Facebook-owned Oculus from this discussion, because those are more obvious.

MEDIA 2.0'S KEY LIVE ACTION VR PLAYERS

JAUNT

Blue chip investors like Google Ventures flocked to immerse their cash into this Bay Area-based company when it launched in 2013 to develop and commercialize its own 360 degree live action VR camera. Jaunt later changed course to focus on VR content, and set up its own LA-based VR production studio in 2015 to pursue those media aspirations. That's when Disney, Sky and other major media companies invested a healthy $65 million more to bring Jaunt's total haul to over $100 million. Cash alone doesn't solve all, of course, and live action VR storytelling at mass commercial scale is challenging to say the least. Jaunt isn't quite there yet, as its experiences likely have yet to significantly monetize. But, that shouldn't be all that surprising, given how nascent the VR space is.

Relatively new CEO George Kliavkoff hopes to change that with his new Media 1.0 buddies and Jaunt's new international joint venture, Jaunt China. Jaunt's powerful media and entertainment allies include Disney, perhaps the greatest storyteller of them all. That creative SoCal Hollywood DNA certainly may hasten closure of the VR language gap for Silicon Valley tech-born Jaunt. As examples, Jaunt released several high-end VR experiences in 2017, including a *Fifty Shades of Grey* immersive experience *(I know, I know, say no more ...)* and *Invisible*, a supernatural series directed by *Bourne Identity* director Doug Liman. Jaunt also announced a new VR series based on the cult action horror movie *Lawnmower Man* at Sundance in 2017, and later struck five more key content deals via the likes of mega-talent agencies CAA and WME.

Ultimately, it remains to be seen whether Jaunt's largely SoCal-based Media 1.0 money will be as patient as NorCal VCs that are accustomed to longer-term technology development and market evolution.

And, the long-term live action VR market opportunity demands nothing if not patience.

NEXTVR

NextVR is another live action-focused VR market leader, and it too has attracted significant investment from traditional media ($120 million), including the venture arms of Comcast and Time Warner (which ultimately, stealthily means AT&T – *yes, there it is again!*). NextVR's focus is to bring live events and sports to life, and its client list is impressive, including Fox Sports, NBC Sports, and Live Nation, with which it will stream hundreds of concerts in virtual reality. It plans to use its cash hoard to deliver more subscription content and unveil more paid events.

HERE BE DRAGONS/WITHIN

From the innovative and iconoclastic mind of Chris Milk, one of the immersive space's most respected creative visionaries, we have two related companies – Here Be Dragons (formerly VRSE) and Within. Here Be Dragons is a VR-driven content studio through and through – no hardware in sight. Discovery Communications fueled it with a $10 million cash injection in August 2017.

Meanwhile, Within is both a distributor of Here Be Dragons content and a content/experience creator itself. The company has raised $56.6 million to date, including a massive $40 million cash infusion in 2017 from the likes of diverse A-players Fox, WPP, WME, Raine Ventures and Andreessen Horowitz to fuel what it calls "spherical filmmaking."

Expect these related companies to help write the live action VR script.

WEVR

WEVR is another SoCal-based VR startup. Its goal is to become the community and YouTube-like home for VR (although YouTube itself hopes to be the YouTube of VR). WEVR also has immersed itself in cash, raising $38.25 million to date, including $10 million from VR headset leader HTC. In addition to serving as a distribution platform for its VR creators,

WEVR produces its own live action VR experiences and counts Lionsgate, among others, as major Hollywood partners.

Are you getting the sense that this VR space is also becoming crowded? That's what I thought.

EMBLEMATIC

Emblematic is yet another SoCal-based immersive company you should know *(See the pattern here? Much of this innovation now comes from LA)*. I hear good things about Emblematic and its quest for VR, AR and MR domination (the company focuses on all forms of immersive). It has a long history of innovation and claims to have developed the first VR documentary, *Hunger*, which premiered at Sundance in 2012 – downright ages ago in the world of Media 2.0. Emblematic's self-proclaimed mission is to be the home of the world's foremost visionaries to create *"fully immersive environments that place the user inside the scene, allowing them to move through, interact, and play with the story."* In other words, to fully develop, flesh out and realize VR's live action entertainment possibilities.

THE VOID

And then there's The Void, based in Salt Lake City – a completely different kind of VR animal than all others on this list *(even its name stands out)*. The Void plays in the out-of-home, location-based entertainment ("LBE") market. Think of The Void as being a VR-driven theme park that takes traditional Disney and Universal Studios experiences to an entirely new, fully-immersive level – way beyond the physical.

The company hopes to capture significant share of the $40 billion plus global theme park market and even broader LBE market. After all, once The Void develops VR experiences, it can easily replicate them on the cheap on small land footprints in shopping malls or any other high traffic zones.

Imagine your very own theme-park-in-a-box, because that's precisely what "it" is. And, these VR black boxes already fill high traffic areas throughout China, a country that is well ahead of the curve in the LBE-focused VR space.

The Void has cleverly "solved" two of VR's greatest challenges – movement and shared, social experiences. The Void participants walk freely, untethered, in its open spaces, wearing vests that carry batteries and processing power, and sensors that deliver 4D vibrations timed in synch with the action to deepen trickery to the mind. And, experiencers actually can "see" and engage with each other via avatars as they participate, making that experience social. Impressive.

You can bet that Disney's Imagineers have been watching, and you'd be right. That's precisely why the Disney Accelerator *(an organization where I served as a mentor)* graciously opened its arms to welcome The Void into its 4th class. Who do you think benefits more from that arrangement? That Disney – smart, smart, smart. As an example, Disney and The Void now work together in developing a new *Star Wars* experience near its theme parks in Anaheim and Orlando.

And, here's the thing. The Void has what neither Disney nor other behemoths have – a seemingly endless supply of cash-rich potential global Media 2.0 mega-partners who themselves are motivated to trap significant share in the global LBE world (and the Mouse in the process). So, don't be too surprised if Disney takes its current relationship with The Void even further into full-fledged acquisition – both as an offensive and defensive maneuver.

INTERNATIONAL

As in any nascent market, the list of live action-focused VR players goes on and on and, of course, includes major international players. Usual suspects include China's BAT companies Baidu, Alibaba and Tencent, each of which is already all-in amidst a Chinese consumer market that buys 40% of the world's VR headsets. Baidu, via its iQIYI streaming video service, announced in 2017 that it intends to build the world's largest Chinese language VR service. The company is investing massively to produce compelling VR content to fuel that consumption. Tencent is also investing "big-ly" in live action VR content, including fully-immersive VR movies and music concert experiences. Meanwhile Alibaba, not surprisingly, focuses first on delivering VR shopping experiences to its hundreds of millions of customers. It fueled adoption of its new form of immersive commerce by giving away Google Cardboard VR glasses, making it easy (maybe too easy!) for VR-laden shoppers to pay for goods with a simple nod of their heads.

Calling all parents, monitor your kids' VR headset use closely (and your credit card bills even more closely)!

Stakes are high. Very. But the VR market opportunity is even higher. You just gotta fearlessly jump into this immersive game.

Chapter 18

● ● ●

AR – SIGNIFICANTLY AUGMENTING ITS EARLY SUCCESS

A R surprised virtually all of us in 2016 – especially after Google's clumsy Glass experiment – when it became a mass cultural phenomenon and everyday reality years ahead of its expected time due to our good old friend Pikachu. *Pokemon Go* became the world's collective *"AHA!"* AR moment, and we downloaded our new little friend 750 million times in its first year. *Pokemon Go* served as the media and entertainment world's early AM *(I mean, AR)* wake-up call.

To virtually all of us, *Pokemon Go* arrived out of the blue, although global treasure hunts, or geocaching, certainly are nothing new. And when it did, the befuddled huddled masses were so obsessed that two of them actually fell off a cliff experiencing it. *(That happened here in my backyard of San Diego where, thankfully, both young men survived with non-life threatening physical injuries, although they likely will continue to suffer deep emotional scars from the very real taunts that most certainly will continue to dog them).*

So, how and why did this phenomenon happen and what lessons can we learn to drive our own Media 2.0 successes?

First, *Pokemon Go* represents the perfect marriage of content and technology to create entirely new and compelling experiences. Its technology doesn't call attention to itself – it is, instead, invisible in the background to bring new experiences to life, which is exactly how the best technology always should be. Google Glass failed a few years earlier because it was not content to hide in the background – it needed to be noticed. Google Glass was all about Google Glass. And, mass consumers just didn't "get" it – either from a "why?" or "how to use?" perspective. *Pokemon Go*, on the other hand, didn't take itself too seriously and was easy and fun to use.

Pokemon Go also tapped into the universal desire to be part of something bigger – a global "moment in time." Here's the thing. Your kids talked incessantly about *Pokemon Go*. So did their friends. So it must be worth checking out, right? And so they did. They then told two friends about it, both via very real-world word-of-mouth and via their even more extensive virtual social channels ... and so on ... and so on ... and so on. Together, they created every marketer's perfect storm.

That brings us to *Pokemon Go*'s third lesson. We all need a little fun and whimsy in the world right now *(where do I begin on that one after the year we had in 2017?)*, and *Pokemon Go* gave us that. With all the dire news that bombards us daily (more like by the minute), flight (escape) is one basic human reaction (desire ... *need?*). Rest the mind. Check out, at least for a few precious Pikachu-enabled moments. A good dose of light-hearted entertainment faire can be just the ticket, especially when that content interacts and actively engages.

Pokemon Go represents the perfect antidote to life's ever-increasing complexity. Bring your tech down a notch by wrapping it up in a friendly package. Apple is notorious for doing this right with its own highly complex products (and takes this lesson even further by making its clean, simple packaging downright "sexy"). Media 2.0 gives you powerful new social media tools to build your own light-hearted, yet very seriously impactful and viral moments. Remember our good friend Dollar Shave Club? Use *Pokemon Go*'s and Dollar Shave Club's lesson of "fun" to increase the impact of your messages. Then, you too at least have the Dos Equis potential to be "the most interesting [brand] in the world." *(Speaking of that brand's notorious marketing campaign, who likes the new guy? Me neither!)*.

Pokemon Go also taps into our fundamental universal human need for actual physical interaction and connection. *"Huh? What? Pokemon Go is AR!"*, you say. *"It's virtual. Not human at all!"* That sounds right, of course. But, think about it. What made *Pokemon Go*, well, "go" is the fact that it became very much a communal experience. Yes, you could experience it on your own. But, for most, it was far more satisfying when shared with others in the real world *(so long as you weren't the ones falling off that cliff)*.

Pokemon Go gave its primarily young, digital native experiencers the best of both worlds. They got to play in their cool new immersive *Pokemon Go* world, but they also got to get out of their heads when doing it. Rather than being solitary and isolating, *Pokemon Go* became communal and participatory. Kids actually ventured outside of their homes and walked, yes walked! Imagine that. Actual physical exercise. Parents liked all of that – and felt better about themselves because of it.

Finally, *Pokemon Go* offered "purpose" – incentives and goals. They may not have been the loftiest of goals, but they worked nonetheless and underscore how simple those goals can be to be effective. Marketers, are you listening? Of course, *Pokemon Go* ultimately is just a game. An experiential one, but still a game. Succeed with certain actions (find PokeStops) and reap the rewards (virtual eggs). What's the lesson here? Gamify your engagement. Add simplicity and whimsy. Your rewards can be virtual eggs for god's sake. I mean, virtual eggs! *Seriously?*

Yes, apparently so.

Ultimately, *Pokemon Go* is yet another powerful wake-up call to action. To not just copy, but experiment, innovate and create new experiences. So, invest heavily in R&D, educate yourselves and your teams about the Media 2.0 forces in which you play, and get to know the companies (big and small) that lead the way. You will learn much from them. These innovators will frequently happily engage with you – perhaps even experiment with you for free *(yes, I said "free")*. Many would cherish the opportunity to work with you in some kind of pilot program. They need you and your content as much as you need them.

Perhaps even more.

Now let's see who some of Media 2.0's leading and most innovative companies are.

MEDIA 2.0'S KEY AR PLAYERS

Research firm Digi-Capital sees AR's mass adoption coming in four major waves that I will use to frame this discussion: (1) mobile AR software; (2) mobile AR hardware; (3) tethered smart glasses; and (4) stand-alone smart glasses. Within this semi-immersive framework, here are some leading players driving today's AR revolution.

NIANTIC

Pokemon Go's creator gets the top spot on this list, because Niantic first revealed AR's mass market, highly commercial potential in 2016. But, what has Niantic done for us lately?

You may think, not much. But, *Pokemon Go* continues to, well, "go." Strongly. It is no mere fad. 65 million consumers continue to play on a monthly basis (likely including some of you reading this). To put things into perspective, all of gamer-giant Activision Blizzard's hit games reportedly add up to 41 million monthly users.

Still, what will be Niantic's next act, er, app?

Well, this year Niantic announced an intriguing new partnership with the Knight Foundation to drive more of us outside into the real world and into our cities via customized *Pokemon Go*-like experiences *(SoCal-based AR startup Animate Objects discussed below is an innovator doing similar things, but plays with even more sophistication)*. In the words of Knight Foundation VP Sam Gill, *"We were excited to see someone who had seemingly cracked the code of how to use this device we're all carrying around to go out and interact with each other."*

Just ponder that statement for a minute. Quite incredible, really. Gill talks about AR used to fuel *actual* reality – in other words, the original "AR."

Yes, parents, that's the world we live in.

APPLE

If mobile AR software represents the first giant wave of mass global AR adoption, then Apple is one of its most massive players with its ARKit iOS platform. That's why it's second on this list. Even before Apple unveiled its new iPhone 8 and double-sided glass X (which I plan to keep out of the slippery hands of my family), hundreds of millions of devices were ARKit-compatible and ready to amaze us semi-immersively. Apple also is widely reported to be testing wearable AR glasses that it plans to bring to market in 2018-2019.

Leading VR/AR analysts, including Robert Scoble and Tim Merel of Digi-Capital, are betting big on Apple ultimately becoming the single most dominant AR force in the world. Merel makes his case this way – Apple's *"end-to-end ecosystem of hardware, software, app store, developers and retail are natural advantages that can't be beaten."*

That's a damn good argument for AR being Apple's "next big thing."

GOOGLE

Of course Google is a major player in this nascent AR game. Its big AR software bet versus Apple's ARKit is ARCore, its new platform for Android phones. Unlike Apple which operates in its own solitary hardware/software closed environment, Google needs friends (its hardware partners) to succeed – just like with Android. Thankfully for Google, it has a lot of friends.

Google, again like Apple, is also focused on AR glasses, which isn't surprising since it invented the widely-mocked v1 Google Glasses in the first place, and now hopes to redeem itself. Google's new "Google Lens" essentially is image search in reverse, empowering us to identify the details of (and data behind) virtually everything we see. Kind of like the "$6 Million Dollar Man" or "Terminator" *(take your pick whether you want to be good guy Steve Austin or bad guy "Ahnold").*

In any event, AR glasses are a massive market opportunity. Conventional eyewear alone is a $130 billion market today.

Will LensCrafters get into the game?

FACEBOOK

Of course Facebook is here too, just like every behemoth. It sees a pile of cash and can't resist jumping into it. Oculus's proud owner naturally is already a leading player, rolling out yet another ARKit competitor – its

AR software platform called "Camera Effects Platform" *(hmm … not sure about that name)* that it distributes to its billions of Facebook Messenger and WhatsApp users.

Facebook, of course, is also hard at work developing its own pair of futuristic glasses that enable you to see virtual objects in the real world. And, you can bet this ain't no mere hobby. After all, Mark Zuckerberg has boldly anointed immersive technologies as being the next major revolutionary computing platform capable of replacing our smart-phones and computers.

So, maybe don't go out and buy that iPhone X just yet!

MICROSOFT

Fellow behemoth Microsoft also plays in the AR space of course, al-though perhaps a bit more quietly and un-sexily than the others (it is Microsoft after all). Microsoft's main AR contender is "HoloLens," an untethered wearable computer that gives users an ability to free-ly roam about as they experience. Non-flashy Microsoft – the tech world's punching bag for years – wants to conquer both the enterprise and consumer AR markets. Its first unit is priced at $3,000, making it enterprise-only at this point. Microsoft announced in 2017 that its next major version will come with built-in artificial intelligence to op-timize hand tracking and object recognition.

Make no mistake, like Facebook, Microsoft believes that AR ultimately will render all PCs, Macs, laptops, tablets and phones "obsolete" *(that's their word, whatever that means)*. And, Microsoft still has plenty of cash and certainly is willing to spend it. In one small example in the immersive space as year-end 2017 approached, Microsoft acquired Comcast-backed social mixed reality company AlstpaceVR to "build the world's pre-emi-nent mixed reality community."

So don't *(scratch that, never!)* count Redmond out. Microsoft is Media 2.0's "Sidler." Remember that *Jerry Seinfeld* character? When you least expect it, Microsoft sidles up next to you and is just "there."

MAGIC LEAP
And then there's privately-held unicorn Magic Leap, perhaps AR's most enigmatic company – tucked away in Florida about as far away as possible from Hollywood and Silicon Valley. The company raised an astounding $1.9 billion to date, including a fresh $502 million Series D round late 2017 at a reported mind-boggling $6 billion valuation ... *and it still hasn't even released a product yet!* Insane, right? Reason overtaken by AR hype? A sign of a coming tech meltdown and apocalypse? An increasing number of incredulous doubters materialized over the course of 2017, demanding that Magic Leap reveal the goods.

But, in defense of Magic Leap's beyond-bullish investors, don't forget AR's projected massive $120 billion-ish market opportunity. And, although few have seen behind Magic Leap's curtain, those fortunate few who have – like *WIRED* magazine – raved *(and then raved some more)*. Magic Leap is said to be developing a potentially society transforming AR headset technology that holds the potential to enable entirely new media and entertainment experiences that far surpass VR. That's why *Lord of the Rings* director Peter Jackson jumped on board *(literally, on Magic Leap's advisory board)*. Near year-end 2017, the company at least offered some kind of clue about the content that it deems worthy for its reported break-through technology when it teamed up with online comics-focused motion book pioneer Madefire *(a company I like and mention earlier in Chapter 12)*.

With its massive financing, Magic Leap, well, leaps over all other privately-financed AR players. How can other startups compete against those virtually unlimited resources? Mega-rounds of capital don't guarantee success, of course, but they certainly don't hurt. That kind of money enables Magic

Leap to grab the land in this AR arms race and hold on tight. It also affords long-term experimentation and patience to "get it right" or at least get noticed in the process.

And, look at the pedigree and diversity of Magic Leap's private multi-billionaires' club of strategic investors. It represents a veritable "Who's Who" of media and technology. Alibaba, Google, Qualcomm, Warner Brothers, and J.P. Morgan all joined the investor party. Respectively, those represent behemoths in (i) international e-commerce and social media, (ii) search and video, (iii) mobile, (iv) content and media, and (v) finance. That's a pretty well-rounded, global blue-chip cast of characters. And, this A-team is committed to freezing out any privately-financed competition and driving mass success across all consumer and enterprise channels with their collective reach and influence.

Formidable. All of us will finally see what all the fuss is about in 2018 when Magic Leap releases its first AR "product," which is said to be bigger than a pair of glasses but smaller than a VR headset. Ultimately, it wouldn't surprise me if one or more of Magic Leap's giant investors ultimately makes a play to buy out the entire company. *"Try before you buy,"* remember?

Alibaba anyone?

META

And then there's privately-held Meta based in the heart of Silicon Valley tech. Like Magic Leap, Meta makes both AR hardware and software. Its self-proclaimed goal is to develop *"a new generation of natural machines that are poised to become a healthy, vital extension of how people create, collaborate and communicate."* But, Meta is trying to accomplish those lofty goals on a comparatively shoestring budget. The company has raised a "mere" $85 million to date, including $50 million from Comcast Ventures and Chinese media-tech giant Tencent.

Unlike Magic Leap or Microsoft's HoloLens, Meta remains tethered to real world computers, a significant disadvantage at least for certain applications like gaming. Perhaps that's why the company is first focusing on enterprise applications. Its reported strengths over HoloLens include a wider viewing area and purportedly more natural interaction with holographic images. But, we all know that "best" doesn't always "win."

Meta is certainly the David to the Magic Leap and other Goliaths discussed above.

8I

8i – which describes itself as being a holographic company – wasn't on my radar last year, but certainly is deserving this year. Its Holo app turns your smartphones into holographic devices that bring your favorite characters into full 360 degree life (a la Princess Leia when she beseeches Obi Wan Kenobi to help her because he is her *"only hope"*). This LA-based startup raised an impressive $27 million in 2017, bringing its total haul to $41 million. Equally impressive, 8i attracted its capital from an international cast of very real and powerful strategic characters to bring its technology to life, including Time Warner, Baidu, Hearst and Verizon.

BLIPPAR

Another AR innovator worth mentioning is Blippar, a mobile-centric visual discovery app backed by none other than mobile global kingpin Qualcomm, among others. It too has a massive cash hoard – in its case $100 million-plus. Blippar started its life essentially as a marketing agency, but pivoted in a big way to leverage its image recognition capabilities to create a visual search engine for the physical world. CEO Ambariash Mitra puts it this way – Blippar wants to be your *"complete visual browser,"* recognizing anything you view with your phone. In other words, a significantly more sophisticated *Pokemon Go,* which uses comparatively rudimentary geolocation to fuel its AR experience.

But, Blippar's mission sounds a lot like the vision of virtually all the behemoths discussed above (including Google Lens), so it certainly won't be easy. Of course, having a big brother like mobile-maven Qualcomm certainly helps. And, thus far, big brands like Coca-Cola, Pepsi, General Mills, Proctor & Gamble, and Nestle have lined up, hoping to mesmerize us all into buying their real products in the real world with very real cash.

ANIMATE OBJECTS

Although small, this San Diego-based company is doing big things, and with a very different focus. Animate Objects takes its market-leading AR technology "ARGO" out into the real world and into the realm of theme parks, live events, and retail – essentially into any physical environment. While ARGO mirrors certain *Pokeman Go*-like characteristics, its technology is far more sophisticated. Partners like Legoland already have implemented the company's features to enhance in-park customer experiences. The potential here is to drive higher customer satisfaction which, in turn, drives higher monetization. After all, we happily spend more when we are feeling good.

But that's not all. Animate Objects' venue partners like Legoland can use ARGO's back-end technology to monitor overall crowd-flow and implement new AR experiences "on the fly" in order to drive customers to other less congested in-venue locations, including on-site retail. That, once again, enhances customer satisfaction and monetization. Partners can super-charge those on-site sales further by using ARGO to deliver guests AR-driven flash offers so that they spend more while being happier and less exhausted.

I like this one. I spent four years in the venue-focused division of Universal Studios and understand the immense problems that ARGO technology can solve, as well as the massive monetization and ROI that can flow from Animate Objects' elegant solutions.

OTHER BEHEMOTHS
Like all other Media 2.0 opportunities, AR is a global phenomenon and this chapter only scratches the surface. As examples, China's Tencent is very much focused both on AR's software layer and AR-friendly entertainment. Alibaba, on the other hand, already has invested massively to be China's immersive e-commerce leader.

Exciting times indeed.

Chapter 19

● ● ●

VR, AR & THE GREAT UNKNOWN

Together, as we have seen in Chapters 17 and 18, VR and AR immersive virtual experiences already deliver meaningful actual realities in our Media 2.0 world. And, much is written about the incredible promise and potential power of immersive technologies for all of us, including those of us in the worlds of media and entertainment. They ultimately will take us places – and enable us to *experience* things – that we can't even fathom right now.

Much less is written in the Media 2.0 industry press about the known and, even more importantly, unknown risks associated with full (or even partial) sensory immersion. These are VR's and AR's great unknowns.

Yes, VR is another way for creators to reach consumers with compelling content. But, it's so much more than "seeing." VR, in fact, is not really a visual medium at all. It is an "experiential" one, and that's not just marketing hype. We aren't so much watching or listening to stories. We are immersed directly in them. VR, unlike purely visual media, generates very real deep physiological and biological impacts – your mind and body actually believe you are experiencing a particular non-virtual reality moment right here, right now. No separation from reality exists. You are simply "present." Presence, in fact, is a concept fundamental to total immersion.

Many tantalizing positives flow from all this, of course.

Enhanced entertainment is an obvious one. You can now actually "be" Obi-Wan Kenobi or Darth Vader inside *Star Wars* (take your pick). Or, even better, really "feel" for those in the experience itself. VR can transport you to anywhere in the world, enable and empower you to get a real sense of what it feels like to be "there" at that particular moment and time. And, that can potentially drive mass empathy and real social impact.

Case in point *Clouds Over Sidra*, an immersive experience created by VR pioneer Chris Milk whom I already have mentioned several times. This experience places you directly in the middle of a Syrian refugee camp, through which you are guided by a 12-year old girl named Sidra. As you experience a day in her life, no longer is being a refugee in some far away land just some mere abstract concept. Now, due to VR's immersive power, Sidra's daunting challenges come to life both in your mind and body in a way that simply "is." And, once Sidra's life becomes more tangible and, therefore, more real to you, then real emotions take hold. Real empathy. Empathy that holds real power and potential to drive real change. To take real action to better the lives of Sidra and others around the world.

Imagine journalists taking that VR-driven empathy machine to cover tragic and catastrophic global events like Mexico's horrific back-to-back earthquakes in 2017 and the continuous, relentless, unprecedented, battering and devastating string of hurricanes in the Caribbean. Who can doubt that our charitable donations and overall mindfulness would substantially increase because of being immersed in the scene and suffering (*even as climate deniers turn their heads away from undeniable climate change realities and the horrific devastation that flow from them*).

Let's take VR's teleportation power a different direction. Global travel. Think of that power for the elderly, the physically-challenged, the under-privileged – those for whom the luxury of travel is simply out of reach. Now all can see the world. Scratch that, *"be"* in that world! Imagine your kid's next field trip. The Travel Channel indeed!

Beyond media and entertainment, but still in the realm of content, imagine experiences for the treatment of health and psychological issues. Firsthand Technology (previously DeepStreamVR) is a VR startup that helps children burn victims cope with pain by immersing them in a VR world of snow, refocusing their bodies and minds. That VR-induced trickery is reported to directly result in pain reductions comparable to that of opiates. Incredible.

Spanish startup Psious is another interesting VR startup changing lives for the better. Its immersive technology develops an exposure therapy tool that helps people cope with debilitating fears of all kind – fear of flying, fear of heights *(perhaps even my fear of writing another book!)*. The company has found that if its patients (for lack of a better word) can experience their particular fears in a controlled environment, they can learn to overcome them.

These examples demonstrate VR's revolutionary potential to enhance quality of life.

But, as with any new technology that holds great promise, serious known – and unknown – risks exist.

In the realm of entertainment, VR takes already-intense horror experiences several extremely scary steps further. Now, you aren't just watching the gore, knowing all the way that you are divorced from it. Outside of it. Now your mind and body actually feel the bloodbath. That you are in-side of it. I've been there. When I first demoed a VR zombie apocalypse experience, my body instinctively recoiled with horror after a ghoul approached me from behind to attack *(okay, I admit it – I actually kind of screamed out loud)*.

Take that even further. Imagine gamer-beloved *Call of Duty*, VR style. You aren't just playing war amidst all of its death and destruction. Your body now feels as if it is at war. The prospect of real trauma is very real indeed. Researchers already study the potential post-traumatic stress disorder impacts of VR. And, some experts believe such experiences may cause actual – even permanent – psychological damage. That's why Alex Schwartz, CEO of leading and now Google-owned VR game developer Owlchemy Labs (developer of popular VR title *Job Simulator*), concludes that VR-driven scares *"are borderline immoral."*

And, that's why many in the industry now push for new content standards for this brave new immersive world. We simply don't yet even come close to understanding the full implications here. We just know that serious questions exist.

So, does that mean we have some kind of moral obligation in terms of how we develop, distribute and experience the immersive possibilities?

Talk amongst yourselves.

Part II, Section 4

● ● ●

OTHER EMERGING MEDIA 2.0 PLATFORMS

Chapter 20

● ● ●

A WORD ABOUT GAMES & ESPORTS

As massive as the theatrical motion picture business is with global box office crossing the $38.6 billion mark in 2016, it pales next to the global games market that reached nearly $100 billion that same year. In the movie business, a $100-$200 million box office opening weekend signals a blockbuster. Multiply that by 10, and you have the game industry's largest opening. In 2013, *Grand Theft Auto V* grossed $800 million in its first 24 hours and hit the $1 billion mark in just three days.

Media and entertainment companies (and storytellers in general) benefit from this relentlessly lucrative market, of course, via lucrative licensing deals. Gamers are hard-core super-users – generally young and male – who certainly aren't afraid to spend money (at least for the games they love). They engage deeply with content and with each other, and like to watch other gamers in action *(hence the Twitch phenomenon I discussed earlier in Chapter 11)*. Gamers love a good head to head challenge, even if they watch it live, online.

Well, guess what? These head-to-head gamer battles on epic games like *Call of Duty* or *League of Legends* have spawned an entirely new industry known as eSports, which is projected to generate billions of dollars worldwide over the next few years. eSports is already far more massive than you may think. Analyst firm Newzoo anticipates that eSports will have reached an audience of 385 million in 2017, including 191 million diehard fans. For several years *(yes, years)*, eSports have already attracted more young male viewers than the World Series or NBA finals. And, analyst firm Activate forecasts that eSports will exceed 10 percent of all U.S. sports viewing and reach 500 million fans worldwide by 2020, significantly more than major traditional sports like basketball.

Just like any real world traditional sport, eSports feature teams of players who compete with each other and become celebrities in their own right with massive social followings, of course. Leading players, like their more traditional star counterparts, become LeBron-like superstars to a digital-native millennial audience that finds them to be more directly relatable. *League of Legends* stage-named superstar Faker, for example, makes $2 million-plus annually, excluding sponsorship revenues *(yes, "excluding" – you heard me right!)*. These super-"e"thletes are increasingly repped by a new breed of management firm like LA-based Cloud9, which raised $28 million from WWE, among others. It's starting to look a lot like "traditional sports." So, it shouldn't surprise you that head to head team competitions now regularly take place in large-scale arenas filled to capacity with tens of thousands of fan-boys.

"But, should eSports really be considered to be a new 'real' category of sports?" you ask. You be the judge. First, let's be clear. eSports isn't entirely new. Video game pioneer Atari held a Space Invaders tournament in 1980 that attracted 10,000 participants. And second, where "real" sports go, gambling always follows. And, analyst firm Narus Advisors estimated that we wagered $5.5 billion on eSports in 2016. That seems real to me.

Brands and advertisers agree and increasingly think of eSports as simply being a new class of sports for a new millennial generation (just like Whistle Sports is a new kind of sports-focused media company for a new digital and social native audience). All the big brand names you know and love, especially highly-caffeinated ones like Red Bull and Coca-Cola, already spend significant sums to sponsor individuals, teams and events. That's why eSports Sponsorship revenues are expected to nearly quadruple to $2.5 billion by 2020.

Smart, bold traditional media and entertainment companies see these unmistakable trends and are moving aggressively into eSports to reach this valuable millennial demographic. In 2017, even Media 2.0-challenged Viacom invested in Super League Gaming, a company known for hosting eSports competitions in movie theaters, as well as online. And, in another notable and more aggressive move one year earlier, Turner Broadcasting partnered with mega-agency WME-IMG to create the first eSports league appropriately called "*ELeague*." Think of it, aspirationally at least, as being the NFL of eSports. Turner now broadcasts eSports events from its ELeague on its very traditional cable channel TBS.

Not to be outdone on its gaming home turf, behemoth Activision Blizzard joined the party, buying live eSports event organizer Major League Gaming in 2016 for $46 million and creating its own eSports league called "Overwatch." Activision's stated quest is to become the "ESPN of eSports." Sound familiar? Meanwhile, ESPN embarked on its own quest to be, well, the ESPN of eSports, by launching its own dedicated eSports channel online and broadcasting tournaments offline. And, underscoring the global and borderless nature of eSports and all of these Media 2.0 opportunities, Chinese behemoth Tencent in 2017 committed to invest $15 billion into eSports over the next five years. Clearly, the virtual has become very real big business that generates very real cash. Lots of it.

And, eSports is not just for existing giants either. You can bet that a long list of startups are also in the game, and you'd be right. Some worth noting include "SLIVER.tv" (a NorCal company that has raised $16 million from Samsung NEXT, Sony Innovation Fund and CAA, among others, to develop a platform to record, view, and stream eSports in fully immersive cinematic VR), "Dojo Madness" (a Berlin-based startup with $12.8 million from The Raine Group, 500 Startups and others to offer a virtual coaching app for competitive gamers that leverages machine learning), "Smash.gg" (another NorCal-based company with $11 million from Accel Partners and Horizon Ventures to host online gaming tournaments), "Gamer Sensei" (a startup that is headquartered in Boston, has raised $6.3 million from Advancit Capital, Greycroft Partners and others to offer an online platform that uses algorithms to match competitive video gamers with "coaches"), and LA-based "Fanai" (which has raised nearly $2 million from Greycroft Partners and others to optimize fan and brand engagement in eSports via an AI-driven monetization platform).

eSports already is a major new Media 2.0 force that is still very much in its early innings. Don't think of it as being a fad, because it isn't. And, its expected hockey stick-like rise – together with the mainstreaming of VR and AR – will only accelerate growth of the already-massive overall games industry that underpins it.

Chapter 21

● ● ●

OFFLINE, LIVE EXPERIENCES
(THE OFT-FORGOTTEN MULTI-PLATFORM PLANK)

This book focuses on our increasingly online virtual world of digital media, not so much on the offline physical world of live experiences. But, in an interesting paradox, our increasingly virtual lives generate a very human *counter*-reaction – an accelerating human desire for real physical interaction, connection and lasting "experiences" in our increasingly technology-driven, ephemeral, and frequently disconnected world. These forces are too frequently overlooked in our Media 2.0 world, but absolutely should be actively considered and implemented in any fully-realized multi-platform strategy.

We still go to the movies, don't we? We still fight traffic and the throngs, and still pay for expensive popcorn when we can watch from the quiet solitude of our own homes. Why? Precisely because we are social creatures, and we don't always want quiet solitude. Have you experienced watching a thriller like 2017's blockbuster "*It*" in a theater and, then, the same thriller at home? "It's" *(yes, pun intended)* an entirely different experience due to the entirely different energy generated in the big communal room versus your smaller private room. It's simply more thrilling to watch a thriller with others who gasp when you gasp and jump when you jump (or even trigger your jumps in the first place).

The virtual and physical worlds absolutely can (and should) be connected in this increasingly disconnected digital world in which we all "communicate" with each other, but frequently question how meaningful that communication is and whether we are part of any real community. Remember *Pokemon Go* from Chapter 18? That's what I'm talking about. And, that's just one rather "small" possibility. Let's think much bigger.

Disney is perhaps the single most multi-platform media company on the planet. The Mouse House practically invented offline real-world live engagement with its theme parks, and now plans to take its vision significantly further. Disney – soon-to-be Netflix's new SVOD arch-nemesis – announced a tantalizing new Media 2.0 initiative in July 2017. Disney revealed that it plans to open immersive *Star Wars* hotels where each guest gets his or her own storyline. Talk about a truly multi-platform experience! Now, *The Force* can be with you anywhere you are – online, in movie theaters, in merchandising, in virtual reality, in theme parks, and now in hotels where the line between where your guest status begins and ends blurs.

And, how about Amazon? As I discuss over and over in this book, this new Media 2.0 juggernaut thinks anything but small. Amazon constantly amazes, especially in its understanding of, and increasingly aggressive action in, a full 360-degree multi-platform strategy that deeply incorporates offline live, real-world human engagement and experiences.

Amazon debuts its motion picture Originals, including Academy Award-winning movie *Manchester By the Sea,* in movie theaters (not online). In another fascinating example of counter-programming, Amazon increasingly builds out and operates Amazon "book" stores across major U.S. shopping malls, while others tear them down. And, in its most audacious 2017 multi-platform move, Amazon acquired Whole Foods to humanize its overall brand and engage more directly with us on the daily. Don't think for a moment that Whole Foods is just about groceries. Amazon undoubtedly will market all of its produce – including its increasingly tasty Media 2.0 content – across its Whole Foods stores and gather even more data about us and our shopping habits all along the way. Think of it as being your very own 360-degree Amazonian journey that brings new meaning to the term "super"-market.

Not surprisingly, visionary Elon Musk absolutely thinks this way *(does the man ever sleep?)*. He, of course, is already "out there" multi-platform-izing in the most audacious and fearless ways – with his Earth-connected Teslas, rocket-lifted SpaceX's and particle-fueled Hyperloops *(which, according to some visionaries whom I trust, are closer than we think in terms of becoming reality and undoubtedly will fully immerse us in content as we travel in "pods" when they are)*. Mid-2017, reports swirled that Tesla's very own new in-car music and media streaming service may be coming to your Model S(oon). Perhaps Apple, which reportedly stopped development of its own autonomous cars in 2017, should finally just buy Tesla and merge their shared stylized hardware/software, offline/online innovation-driven DNA. Could this really happen? Yes, I really think so. In fact, I predicted this all the way back in 2013 (and have the blog post to prove it).

All these examples demonstrate that what we have here, ladies and gentlemen, is a virtuous cycle of increasingly online/virtual social interaction that fuels the growing movement of offline/physical and downright tribal live real-world engagement – that, in turn, fuels more ongoing online social interaction, action and impact – and then back again. Welcome to our new truly multi-platform Media 2.0 virtuous cycle and overall *Zeitgeist*. Welcome to holistic, 360 degree storytelling.

Let's first take the business of music where, as we saw in Chapter 13, disruption rules the day and traditional revenue streams wither. All doom and gloom, right? Wrong. Music festivals sprout up everywhere *(I am obsessed with them).* Why? Because these festivals become so much more than the music itself. The music draws you in, but the real magic comes from the like-minded community and shared immersive experience created during that moment in time. "Experience" is the key word – and result – here. Experiences and shared humanity are lasting. Those who tried to stop that transcendent magic in 2017 are not. To hell with them.

Rick Farman, co-founder of Superfly (producers of Bonnaroo and Outside Lands, two of the largest U.S. music festivals) strongly agrees. In my conversation with him, Farman describes the need for actual live physical connection as being *"the thirst for high-touch, authentic real-world experiences as people increasingly immerse themselves in the digital world." You have a symbiotic relationship here,"* says Farman. *"Social media helps drive the communal aspects of these very social events, and mobile takes it to another level and amplifies it – driving the whole phenomenon of FOMO."*

Live Earth co-founder and Executive Producer Kevin Wall, an intensely creative media visionary and activist who has created and produced many of the largest live events the world has seen, adamantly agrees. *"Festivals use digital as a driver, but they are anti-digital in what they represent,"* he tells me.

So, how many digitally-driven content companies get it right and fully embrace their physical alter-ego? Not many.

On the music side, we now know that Spotify's and Pandora's challenges are daunting (to say the least), and that they must either significantly diversify their businesses or be acquired to survive. One part of that solution may be to bring their online customer engagement into the physical world of music festivals. Expand their brand into the real world in order to expand their overall connection (brand love) with their otherwise rather anonymous customers. Deepen them. Create a real differentiated and fully realized community. The Pandora "Unboxed" Music Festival! *"Gold*

Jerry, Gold!" Again, the online virtual community drives more offline participation and success which, in turn, drives more (and more continuous) online engagement and success.

It goes the other way too. Hey, music festivals, harness the energy from your magical weekends that typically dissipates when the weekend is over. Mobilize that passionate community you created. Continue its life and extend that energy online. Continue the conversation and almost-tribal sense of community beyond the physical venue itself via virtual interaction and social media. You'll be glad you did. So will your investors. You have the new Media 2.0 tools to drive success like never before. KAABOO, the major music festival that just completed its successful third year in my backyard of San Diego, smartly thinks this way.

Now let's take video. How about Netflix, the granddaddy of the OTT video space? Yes, Netflix is the category leader. But, as I discuss throughout this book, it too faces its own existential business model challenges. Netflix's customer experience is all virtual. Why shouldn't Netflix try to differentiate itself from its increasing list of behemoth competitors (like Amazon, Google/Youtube, AT&T and Apple) that have fundamentally more diverse business models? Why not bring the Netflix brand and experience into the physical world much like Apple did with its stores – and Amazon smartly is doing with its new "book stores" and Whole Foods? That may mean differentiated Netflix stores. But, it also may include Netflix-driven theater experiences (again, Amazon is already there), Netflix-branded community screenings, film festivals. Myriad possibilities exist.

After all, online video services like Netflix gather deep user data of like-minded viewers in cities across the country. If any of these premium video services successfully create physical communities under their individual banners, then they can leverage these new offline experiences to drive further and magnified success online.

These are just some ideas – some concepts – that hold the potential to be transformative. Perhaps these concepts spark some ideas of your own in your own personal quest to be fearless.

Action, remember? Not merely reaction. Or, even worse no action at all.

Chapter 22

● ● ●

SOCIAL IMPACT & MEDIA 2.0'S UNPRECEDENTED POWER TO DO "GOOD" (THE STEALTH PLANK, RISING ...)

Okay, I've now essentially covered all main individual "planks" that, together, build a holistic, 360-degree Media 2.0 multi-platform vision and strategy.

But, now it's time for a very different and more ethereal plank – Media 2.0's unprecedented power and potential to reach, activate and motivate us to do "good." To generate real positive societal impact on a mass global scale. Consider this one a "stealthy" plank that can be overlaid on top of all the others, and hearkens back to themes from decades past that are making a comeback. And, if you use this one right then, man, you really have something! A virtuous – truly virtuous – cycle of online/offline/connection and impact. *This* is when your multi-platform vision becomes fully realized in the deepest sense.

That is precisely what renown global music event producer Kevin Wall *(discussed earlier in Chapter 21)* had in mind with *Live Earth 2* in 2015 – to mobilize one billion voices, all committed to urging world leaders to take real action to address climate change. How? Wall created a 360-degree campaign that inspired and activated millennials around the world to leverage their collective reach, power and virtual might via all available channels (social, mobile) to connect with each other and send messages directly to world leaders and influencers. The actual physical *Live Earth 2* festival served as the climax to that multi-platform campaign and was, of course, televised to a global audience *(traditional platform, activated)*.

And, you know what? It worked! Wall's ambitious, audacious campaign not only achieved its goals, that overwhelming wave of Media 2.0-enabled mobilization also served as a clarion wake-up call to global leaders, reminding them that the world's youth were watching. That global microscope, in turn, motivated essentially every single global leader to finally take action and sign the unprecedented Paris Climate Accord. Media 2.0 enabled this collective action. Media 2.0 fueled it. Media 2.0 empowered the people.

And then the Trump happened ....

Well, let's take that back. Do any of you reading this really doubt that 2017's consecutive cataclysmic hurricanes are a direct result of climate change? Let's build a wall! A new Kevin Wall-inspired *Live Earth 3* movement that refuses to accept denials and deniers. And, let's use all of Media 2.0's planks to get us there.

Or, how about this? Several of Media 2.0's top young creators and influencers – including Lilly Singh and Lizzie Velasquez *(both properly honored at The Streamy's inspiring 2017 inaugural "Purpose Awards" that I was fortunate to attend)* – use their massive global social platforms to educate their tens of millions of millennial followers about global causes and crises and to motivate them to take real action and be part of the "solution." To volunteer. Contribute. Be aware. Inclusive. Or, just plain be positive, respectful and "good." You know, basic human elements of decency too often missing in the course of our everyday discourse *(especially from that same 1600 Pennsylvania Avenue address)*.

And those positive actions breed more positive actions that, in turn, seep into and transform society's overall D.N.A. That's happening right now. I see it everywhere. Doing "good." Standing up (or kneeling down) for what's right. Those have become central priorities of our younger generations that, studies show, carry real significant dollar value (as in, earning less money, but giving more and achieving more lasting fulfillment). *(Calling all you Millennials – don't forget to go offline to your nearest voting booth in 2018 – you know, don't forget the "live venue" plank!)*.

That's the power of Media 2.0 storytelling. A compelling message can reach virtually all of us at any given moment in time, and just about anywhere on this planet. We can now, for the first time, take immediate action from our phones. We are moved by a video or immersive experience (like Chapter 19's *Clouds Over Sidra*) and then, with a few taps on our phone, we can immediately donate to hurricane relief, sign up to volunteer to ease suffering, or sign an online petition demanding more immediate governmental action. We can even create our own stories and immediately inject them into the global conversation. Now that's democracy in action! That's precisely the vision of crowd-funding platform GoFundMe, which established a new video production studio late 2017 to mobilize action and giving via stories of empathy and compassion.

These are the transformational themes that serve as the very foundation of the *Life is Beautiful* music, arts and education festival in Las Vegas (themes that will never die in Vegas, or anywhere else). That's the mission of Media 2.0 startup "Good Amplified," a multi-platform media company dedicated to showcasing and promoting non-profits, foundations, and these overall ideals. And, similar impactful (yet still highly commercial) themes drive the mission of new media company Uproar, a new media company focused on wildlife and conservation for the mobile generation.

Just three examples of a growing movement in Media 2.0's new world order.

In the words of Nobel Prize winning poet Bob Dylan, *"The times, they are a changin'...."*

Part III

• • •

MEDIA 2.0 NEWS YOU CAN USE

Chapter 23

● ● ●

MEDIA 2.0'S TOP 10 LESSONS

Because we now live in a technology-infused BuzzFeed-ian world of short attention spans and "listicles," here are my Top 10 key takeaways – and even some concrete ideas – that flow from the previous chapters and may help you define your overall business strategies (especially those of you in traditional media who may need to fundamentally transform your way of thinking amidst Media 2.0 realities). In true David Letterman fashion *(one of my Media 1.0 heroes who now plans to make a comeback on Netflix at a price tag of $2 million per episode)*, I start with lesson #10 and work my way down to the single most important lesson of them all, which should now be obvious.

Cue the drumroll, please.

LESSON #10 – The Internet and technology have changed everything about engaging with an audience – content development, content marketing, content distribution, and content monetization. Hey, traditionalists! This means you need to re-think essentially everything about your media business ... and then re-think it again. Heed these sage words spoken by Disney Chairman & CEO Bob Iger at a September 2017 industry conference. *"I think the most important thing one has to do* *when they're contending with change is to admit that it's occurring and to assess very carefully what the impact of the change is on all the businesses,"* he told the crowd. Amen to that. And, that kind of re-thinking includes who is actually doing the thinking for you. Do they have the right background and digital DNA?

Hire young, hungry new Media 2.0 talent (social media experts, engineers and the like) and the right experienced advisors to accelerate your company's learning. My team and I work with both traditionalists and new entrants all the time to extend their in-house capabilities, uncover and deliver proprietary market intelligence they can't find anywhere else, and map out new digital transformation strategies to stay ahead of competitors and maximize their opportunities.

Here are four concrete examples of how companies engaged with CREATV Media and my teams as trusted advisors: (1) we interviewed key industry leaders to gain insights otherwise not available to a leading digital-first media company; (2) we internally analyzed a leading traditional Hollywood production and management company, conducted a full forensic of the industry in which they sit, helped them identify new growth opportunities, and laid out a full strategic execution plan to hasten their digital transformation and build enterprise value; (3) we advised one of the major studios on overall industry trends, where the Media 2.0 business is today (across all major market categories, including those covered in this book), where those markets are going, and how precisely they can actively and smartly get into the game both directly and via partners (and even identified potential partners); and (4) we traveled overseas to advise a foreign governmental trade and investment organization, as well as several international business delegations, on the overall Media 2.0 industry and to identify new opportunities for them to participate and profit in it – essentially serving as a "Bridge to Hollywood" to identify key U.S.-based executives and companies with which they could partner (and then to facilitate such transformational partnerships).

LESSON #9 – The speed of change and technological advancement is only increasing. That means you should increasingly invest in studying it, including the key players and what they are doing. Challenge yourself to stay ahead of it, as well as the competition that is increasingly trying to do the same. Task your digital transformation-focused team and top advisors to identify some of the most promising Media 2.0 companies. Conduct pilot programs with them. Demo days. Trust me, those innovators will be thrilled to participate and likely won't even charge you for it.

CREATV Media is frequently called into action to do just that – identify the most innovative young companies with which they can partner, experiment and learn, as well as immerse them in intensive highly-curated sessions and workshops that showcase those innovators in action, together with their products and services. My team and I have organized several of these kinds of events, which frequently feature multiple "under the radar" companies exclusively demo-ing their wares. There is nothing like actually experiencing something new for the first time. That's frequently how the fire starts.

Or, identify some of the most compelling Media 2.0 companies before your competitors do and strategically invest in them in order to get your feet wet and learn, learn, learn. Even bolder, start a digital/tech-focused incubator internally – essentially an R&D lab with innovative companies that apply to be part of it. Fox did just that with the Fox Innovation Lab, Disney did it with its Disney Accelerator, and innovative media/tech law firm Stubbs, Alderton & Markiles did it with its highly respected seed-stage "Preccelerator" *(Well done Stubbs!)*. To the rest of you, if lawyers can do it, you can too *(no slam on lawyers, since I too was once a member of that club)*. If nothing else, those kinds of moves send an important message to your company, employees, investors and the world that you take the disruptive Media 2.0 forces that engulf you seriously and are taking real, concrete action to use them to your game-changing advantage.

I know from personal experience that these kinds of innovative bets really work. Major media companies regularly work with CREATV Media to identify the most compelling Media 2.0 opportunities in which to strategically invest. In one example, we facilitated traditional media investment of over $20 million in one Media 2.0 company that has since become the leading player in its market segment. In another, we facilitated an initial early-stage investment by a leading Asian conglomerate into a new media content category killer.

LESSON #8 – Data matters, is incredibly valuable, and can be a game-changer for you. Internet and technology-driven market intelligence should inform your strategies, decisions and customer engagement like never before (and can also add a critical feedback loop). If you don't capture data – and measure everything – then you ain't doing it right. Be a hero. Spend time to identify new data capture, measurement and analytical tools and companies, and experiment with them. You likely will be surprised by the enlightening information you see, but really was there all the time and simply masked by preconceived traditional Media 1.0 notions.

CREATV Media works with companies to understand Media 2.0's possibilities and identify the leading data players in the marketplace, so that they can build on top of industry best practices and immediately add real, significant ROI as a result of those efforts.

LESSON #7 – The Internet has made the world truly global, borderless, connected. The opportunity to expand and monetize your reach is here and now. Seize it, and don't feel the need to go it alone. Partner with like-minded international media companies and technology innovators to speed your path. Conduct a deep, thorough overall market and competitive landscape market assessment to identify the right ones. And then connect efficiently.

This is something CREATV Media does all the time for companies big and small, domestic and international. We know the marketplace, are very close to leading executives, entrepreneurs and influencers in it, identify potential target partners for outreach, connect our clients with those targets at the highest decision-making levels, and then help structure and execute new game-changing partnerships.

Here are just three examples that may be instructive to kick off your own efforts: (1) we recently introduced one of the major U.S.-based media companies to the CEO of the largest mobile-first media company in Southeast Asia, a company which otherwise would have stayed under its radar; (2) we connected a major international trade organization to key innovators in the Media 2.0 landscape based here in the U.S.; and (3) we worked with an organization representing major Chinese media companies to identify compelling U.S. content that they could license from leading Hollywood studios to feature on their own services.

LESSON #6 – We now live in a multi-platform world, where mobile has become the single most important screen and universal connection point. Mobile gives the tantalizing opportunity to reach and engage with virtually any consumer on the planet at any time, 24/7. Embrace this reality – and massive potential opportunity – and craft your strategies of engagement with mobile top of mind. This lesson is especially true to reach millennials, the audience marketers most want to reach. If you don't "get" this, then just look at the kids around you and see what they are doing.

CREATV Media regularly works with companies across the Media 2.0 ecosystem to identify specific mobile-driven opportunities – including innovative mobile-first creators, studios and content, as well as the mobile-driven services and technologies that support and proliferate them. In the former case, as an example, my firm now represents a highly profitable leading mobile-first studio that efficiently develops premium fact-based content in multiple languages. And, as an example of the latter, we represent an innovative new mobile-focused AR technology platform that works with major venues like theme parks to enhance customer experiences and drive new revenue streams.

LESSON #5 – Our increasingly mobile-first world demands deep mobile-first engagement, and that is frequently best-driven by video. Video is the language of mobile, and your customer engagement and execution strategies should reflect that reality. This edict applies to virtually all companies in the Media 2.0 ecosystem, no matter what size (yes venture capitalists, even to you). High quality video production and hosting are now drop dead easy and cost effective. Tell your stories, visually. Feature them on your website and in social media. If done right, then your followers will do the rest of the work for you.

At the same time, don't completely reject "old" forms of media – like basic text itself. Reinvent them for a new heads-down mobile audience. There is a reason we all text so feverishly after all, so how about new bite-sized, snackable mobile mini-narratives like those offered by Wattpad and Yarn?

This all takes time, of course – to study what's out there, available and working in the marketplace to accomplish your goals. Again, this is where CREATV Media is frequently called into action to do the studying based on our industry expertise. To give an objective and unbiased industry insider's analysis and bring "the outside, in." And then to make the connections needed for a company to be off to the races, smartly – guiding it all along the way so that the company doesn't feel like it has been thrown to the Media 2.0 wolves.

LESSON #4 – All media is (or at least has the potential to be) social, particularly in our always-on mobile-first world. And remember, if

your audience finds your content compelling, they will be your most effective marketing channel. So, invest deeply in social. Hire young, hungry social media mavens, agencies, and advisors like CREATV Media to craft your new positioning and execute an effective social media strategy that is fully integrated into your overall multi-platform marketing and engagement strategy and authentic to your brand.

"Authenticity" is the guiding word here. Gotta be true to your voice. Audiences are savvy and getting savvier.

LESSON #3 – Closely related to one of Lesson #9's, well, lessons (the one about establishing Demo Days with young innovative Media 2.0 companies), study what the kids are doing. Watch them. Listen to them (yes, actually listen to them – don't assume you know). They are the best Petri dish to discover and understand new technologies, new services, new ways to engage that are gaining traction with coveted audiences and can potentially be leveraged in exciting new ways. Remember what Brian Robbins' kids did for him. They led him to create AwesomenessTV, which he later sold for $115 million in less than three years. What have your kids done for you lately?

So, start a focus group program to formally inject this priority into your company's DNA. Or at least just spend some real time at the dinner table with your kids. They'll tell you what's happening out there *(am not joking, you will learn a lot – I certainly have from my two teens, who serve as a key part of my R&D team – can't let those valuable resources go to college!).* And, you'll get closer to them by prioritizing that precious and fleeting family time over and over again.

LESSON #2 – History does repeat. New technologies have always disrupted the media and entertainment industry's status quo – television disrupting radio, the Betamax later threatening television and

the movies (you know the drill). But the overall business of media and entertainment evolves and always comes out significantly stronger and more deeply engrained – albeit transformed – in our daily lives. Despite the significant pain felt by many to date as a result of our Media 2.0 revolution, the overall media and entertainment ecosystem's pie will grow. Massively.

Remember, the U.S. recorded music industry just enjoyed yet another period of double-digit growth at the hands of streaming, and Goldman Sachs now forecasts the overall global music marketplace to balloon from $15.7 billion to $40-plus billion by 2030. OTT video streaming services proliferate worldwide and direct-to-consumer distribution points are "always open." And, as discussed throughout this book, we have only barely begun to leverage Media 2.0's transformational possibilities.

So, don't be blind to this history. Learn the language of Media 2.0 and believe that Media 2.0 will follow this path. Communicate your newly-transformed lexicon, confidence and overall priority across your teams to set the overall tone. I can't stress enough how critical it is to do this. Better to be positive than negative in any event, because you certainly won't stop this train. It's going with or without you. So, where do you want to be?

My team and I at CREATV Media work with a wide variety of Media 2.0-related players who understandably feel uncertain about their company's position in the overall "space" and recognize that they are sub-optimizing their overall opportunities (some of which may be game-changing but currently out of sight). These include CEOs, directors and entrepreneurs of successful privately-held companies, as well as leading executives of major studios (sometimes even governmental organizations). We undertake a full-on strategic "forensic" process that has proven, time and time again, to immediately lead to millions of dollars (even tens of millions of dollars) of enhanced enterprise value in the eyes of external potential strategic partners simply because the company engaged in this optimization process.

In other words, that company is perceived differently – and is valued significantly more – by the marketplace (including potential strategic partners, investors and even buyers), simply because it now uses the "right" Media 2.0 language and vision to take its current pieces, better position them today, and use them to lay out a credible and compelling course for tomorrow. The ROI on this process is immediate, real, tangible, and proven to be significant – frequently, even invaluable – simply by making an investment of weeks.

Our proprietary process essentially goes like this: (i) we conduct a deep internal evaluation (scrubbing) of a company's current business (team, product, services, customers, partnerships, business model, marketing) and overall positioning within its relevant industry *(we have been successful operators ourselves that have returned high returns for our investors)*; (ii) we identify and understand new market forces and other external factors to understand how the relevant company "fits" within the broader market *(based on our deep industry expertise and proprietary access to critical information)*; (iii) we "place" the company within that broader market and identify potential game-changing opportunities that are ambitious, yet attainable, in order to help management chart their forward-looking strategy and maximize their company's overall enterprise value *(again, based on our unique industry expertise and "neutral" position)*; (iv) we optimize the company's positioning and overall identity consistent with management's new strategy, so that their teams can effectively communicate them out to both internal and external stakeholders *(and we frequently help them communicate that messaging out both to their internal teams and to key industry press and influencers)*; and (v) we help identify and introduce new potential strategic partners to help them get there, faster (some of which, again, may lead to new strategic investment and even M&A) *(we have done this successfully several times not only for our clients, but for ourselves in our own businesses)*.

Trust me, it works. And we have the case studies and testimonials to prove it.

LESSON #1 – It is time for action, not reaction! Don't reject the obvious forces around you – like a slow-down or steady decline in your traditional business, or increased competition that is cannibalizing your opportunities – simply for fear of not doing it right or disruption to your long-standing business model. Financial projections not penciling out? Maybe your traditional assumptions just don't work in today's Media 2.0 world. Remember, no one has it all figured out. Few, if any, have defined the perfect business model.

But, you absolutely must be in the game – boldly! Experiment with new distribution models, marketing and monetization strategies. Iterate. Partner. Buy. Aggressively hire the right Media 2.0 executives and advisors to chart the course. Establish the new rules of the Media 2.0 game.

Heed the cautionary tales of the ghosts of Media 2.0 past – the Blockbusters of the world – that failed to internalize and act upon these lessons (especially this Lesson #1). Tremendous opportunity awaits, but you must actively seize it and put yourself out there.

Boldly. Tenaciously. Relentlessly.

FEARLESSLY!

That's what this book is all about.

Chapter 24

● ● ●

MEDIA 2.0 INVESTMENT AND M&A: ISSUES TO BE CONSIDERED FOR BOTH SIDES

(by Greg Akselrud, Partner
Stubbs Alderton & Markiles and SAM CREATV Ventures)

In the previous chapter, and throughout this book, Peter identifies strategic investment and M&A as being two weapons in Media 2.0's "fearless" arsenal that companies frequently use to take bold transformational action in order to achieve game-changing and game-winning results.

That kind of strategic activity frequently is based in L.A. And with the accelerating pace of that kind of strategic and venture capital investment – and with a similarly accelerating number of Media 2.0-related M&A exits that include mega-deals AT&T/Time Warner ($85 billion), Apple/Beats ($3 billion), Facebook/Oculus ($2 billion), and Disney/Maker Studios ($675 million) – we thought it was time to consider those deal-related issues.

Ladies and gentlemen, it's time for "news you can use," deal edition!

I. INVESTMENTS – JUSTIFYING VALUE

In the ever-changing landscape that is Media 2.0, media and technology companies and investors continue to endlessly debate and negotiate value and valuations – how much is a company "worth." For investors, the formerly frothy investment bubbles have come and gone and fewer unicorns can be found. They thus push for the lowest valuation possible in order to get a larger stake in the company. Founders, on the other hand, of course negotiate for the highest valuation possible – to preserve control, limit dilution and set a baseline value for their idea. The question always arises – how do you justify value?

Without revenue, cash flow or EBITDA *(a widely-used acronym-ian measure of profitability that stands for "earnings before interest taxes depreciation and amortization")* – and many times without projections or even a revenue generating business model – value cannot be calculated based on numbers alone. Accordingly, the key characteristics that justify value end up being: (i) the strength of the management team; (ii) the disruptive nature of the company's business; (iii) market comparables (if they exist); and (iv) investor demand and scarcity. The more experienced the team (having one or more significant exits), the more disruptive the technology, the higher the valuations of other related or comparable market participants, and the more investors desire to invest and feel that they may lose out – the higher the valuation. Conversely, an inexperienced team with little investor demand, even in a strong environment for market participants, will end up with a lower valuation.

Take for example the anonymous messaging app "Whisper." In 2014, the company had drawn comparisons to Snapchat, Yik Yak, and other fast-growing communications apps. As a result, it drew a $200-million valuation and more than $60 million in funding, including from prominent Silicon Valley venture capital firms Sequoia, Lightspeed Venture Partners, and Shasta Ventures. Whisper was able to justify its lofty valuation based on, among other things, the extraordinary value of other key market participants, a then-growing trend in anonymous messaging, and the experience of at least one of its founders, Brad Brooks (who serves as the Chairman of Whisper and the CEO of TigerText). However, in 2017, even with 30 million monthly unnamed users, Whisper authorized a financing at a value that was flat to its earlier 2014 round – demonstrating the changing market landscape and confidence in Whisper's execution.

No matter what, I always advise my company clients that it is better to have a majority of "something" versus 100% of "nothing," which is to say – negotiate the valuation as best you can and stand firm to your vision and perception of value. But at the end of the day, take the best deal you can and give your business a chance to succeed, without over-worrying about how much extra dilution it will cost you.

II. INVESTMENTS FROM STRATEGICS

When looking for potential investors, companies tend to always seek out the usual suspects – friends and family, accelerators, angel investors, and venture capital firms. One target group that is often ignored is strategic investors. Strategic investors are typically larger participants in the target market that, in many cases, operate investment arms that look to make strategic investments in companies. While founders frequently consider these market participants for potential revenue-generating deals like co-marketing, co-branding and distribution – all of which are great – they many times ignore the fact that these strategics may often be in a position to offer so much more via direct investment.

While revenue-generating deals can add significant strategic value as well, they may not actually generate the revenue needed for the company to grow (at least in the short term). That makes the need for investment just as critical, whether from the strategic investor or someone else. Some great examples of strategic investment include Tencent's investment and ultimate acquisition of Riot Games, HTC's original investment in Beats

Electronics, ITV's investment in New Form Digital, and WPP's investment in 88 Rising (a company in which my fund SAM CREATV Ventures is also an investor).

A. ADVANTAGES

In many cases, strategic investors add significantly more value over traditional investors, so long as founders are able to capture some of that value through typical business arrangements – distribution, marketing, and revenue-generation. The value is obvious. First, having a big name strategic investor on the capitalization table (the document that identifies all company shareholders) provides validation for your company/business/idea. It demonstrates to the broader market that this strategic investor has done its due diligence and believes there is adequate value in your company to invest its own money.

Operationally, strategic investors are in most cases larger, well-capitalized, multi-national companies that are able to bring resources to the early stage company (office space, headcount, legal and business affairs, tax planning, etc.). Strategics also are generally able to facilitate broader marketing initiatives and drive more significant distribution and revenue due to platforms and market access that early stage start-ups can't match with their own resources. In fact, in many territories outside the United States, it is extraordinarily difficult to enter a market without a local partner. In those markets, a strategic investor can help open doors, initiating international market expansion that would have been otherwise unachievable or at a minimum, cost prohibitive.

B. DISADVANTAGES

With all of these advantages, there are of course disadvantages. Strategic investors willing to invest in an early stage company want something too. They see the value that the founders have created and want to take advantage. The "asks" by a strategic investor will always vary, but they will most times relate to the following: (i) preemptive rights to invest (essentially the right to invest more and, therefore, increase their ownership percentage in the company before others); (ii) exclusive distribution or advertising rights, or at a minimum, a "first look" or other right of first negotiation on distribution and advertising; and (iii) in some cases, the right of first negotiation to buy the whole company. All of these items are disadvantages because they limit the company's later strategic alternatives.

So, even if it may make sense to involve a big name venture capital fund in a later financing, a strategic investor's preemptive right to invest could eliminate that opportunity. Similarly, the strategic investor may not have the best distribution platform in Latin America, for example. But, if that strategic has an exclusive right to distribute internationally, then the company is stuck with that option. In some cases, even the very existence of a strategic investor on the company's capitalization table is a disadvantage, because it either prohibits the strategic investor's competitors from investing or doing business with the company, or scares off those competitors that may believe a nemesis has already poisoned the well.

In most cases, however, the advantages of having a strategic investor far outweigh the disadvantages, especially if a related commercial business deal is structured to consider and give more flexibility to the company's later-stage strategic alternatives.

As such, it makes a lot of sense for founders to look for these types of investors.

III. CONVERTIBLE SECURITIES – SAFES VS. CONVERTIBLE NOTES

The collective use of convertible securities (or "SAFEs" – simple agreement for future equity) and convertible promissory notes has grown in the early stage start-up investment market, and in some cases, in later investment rounds as well. In many cases, these instruments make sense for both companies and investors. They allow the company to accept investment capital without having to determine and agree upon its current valuation, and they give investors a benefit for making an early investment – essentially a conversion right into the next preferred equity financing at a discounted valuation or a fixed rate of return on a "change of control" (most typically, a company sale). The key difference between these two kinds of structured investments is downside protection. Convertible securities (SAFEs) have no downside protection for the investor, while convertible notes, being traditional debt instruments, do.

A. BENEFITS OF BOTH STRUCTURES

Several important benefits flow from these structures. First, they are much less complicated than a preferred stock financing, while still providing some benefit to the early investor over a straight common stock investment. A preferred equity financing involves adopting an entirely new class of preferred stock, thinking about what rights it should have, and signing 1-4 additional agreements depending on the complexity and sophistication of the round. All of that takes time and incurs legal cost – both of which the company simply may not have.

Second, from a business perspective, the company and investors in many cases either don't know what the valuation for the company should be at the time of investment, or cannot agree on that valuation. In both cases, the parties may still want to get the deal done because they understand that the company may need the money immediately. So these types of structures provide that necessary stop-gap between a basic common stock financing and a more complicated preferred stock financing.

B. COMMON FEATURES

So what do these investment structures have in common? They both provide a structure for an investor to invest now, with the right to receive some benefit in the future – either in the next preferred equity round of financing or in a change of control, whichever comes first.

For the next investment round, these structures typically provide a mandatory conversion provision that requires the principal amount invested in the SAFE or convertible note and interest (if any) to convert into the shares issued in the company's next preferred equity financing (sometimes preferred and common stock) at a discount to the next round, typically between 10-30%.

So as a basic example, (1) if an investor invests $100,000 in the SAFE or convertible note and (2) the discount provided in the SAFE or convertible note is 20% and (3) the next round's preferred equity is being sold at $1.00 per share, then (4) the investor's $100,000 investment would convert into the preferred shares being issued in the next round at a price per share of $0.80. In effect, the investor gets more shares in the preferred equity round as a benefit for having made the earlier investment.

The discount presents itself in mainly two ways – either as a straight discount as described above, or in the form of a "valuation cap" which states that the SAFE or convertible note will not convert at a price per share that is higher than the price per share inferred by that valuation cap (i.e., an agreed maximum valuation for the company divided by the number of shares outstanding immediately prior to the financing). If that number is lower than the price per share derived by the straight discount in the example above, then the investor would be entitled to that lower price per share. This mandatory conversion provision is only triggered if the company raises some minimum amount of money in the next preferred investment round, and that minimum is typically agreed by the company and the investor in advance.

In a change of control, both structures typically provide that the investment amount can convert prior to the change of control at some baseline valuation (usually the valuation cap) or, at the option of the investor, that investor can choose to be repaid some minimum amount which is often 2X the amount invested.

C. KEY DIFFERENCES

The differences between these two structures are straightforward. While the convertible note is a basic debt instrument that accrues interest and requires repayment at an agreed maturity date, a SAFE is a piece of paper, literally. SAFE documents typically do not incur interest and do not contain a maturity date. So, if a company never raises the next preferred equity financing and if there never is a change of control, then the investor in the SAFE will not receive anything and will remain stuck in its SAFE investment indefinitely. While in most cases that result means the company failed, it could also mean that the company had become moderately successful – never having to take in additional investment – but also not worthy of an acquisition.

On the other hand, convertible notes accrue interest and must be repaid at some point. That obligation to repay essentially keeps founders' "feet to the fire," requiring them to find alternatives to raise capital, seek a change of control, or potentially simply just repay the convertible notes.

Companies typically prefer SAFEs/convertible securities, and investors typically prefer convertible notes. But, both structures provide a great path to accomplish a financing.

IV. M&A – BRIDGING THE VALUATION GAP WITH AN EARNOUT

In M&A transactions, like in equity investment transactions, there is always negotiation on valuation. The seller company, like the company in an investment transaction, wants the highest valuation possible. On the other hand, the buyer/acquirer, like the investor in an investment transaction, wants the lowest valuation possible – to either purchase the selling company for less or to hold a larger stake. While transactions can take many forms (a merger, sale of assets or sale of stock) and can involve different forms of consideration (cash, debt or equity), the underlying valuation is always the most important part of the negotiation.

A. VALUATION MODELS

M&A participants use different valuation models to arrive at a mutually agreed valuation. Valuation models include: (i) multiples of EBITDA; (ii) multiples of revenues; and (iii) an analysis of discounted cash flow (i.e., the present value of future cash flow). In some cases where a target seller has not yet achieved revenues or EBITDA – or where preparing accurate projections may be difficult – buyers and sellers do the same thing as companies and investors in investment transactions. They look at the target seller's most important performance metrics (like number of users, market leadership, strength of the management team, etc.), as well as comparable transactions in the market and relative buyer demand.

In entertainment and digital media, typical multiples for production companies and other market participants are generally in the range of 4-8X EBITDA, while revenue multiples vary significantly between as much as 2X and 10X (and sometimes even greater). All of these multiples are unfortunately not formulaic and depend on a host of other factors. For example, a company that mostly offers services that are dependent upon the services of a few individuals may yield a lower valuation multiple than a company that manages a robust technology platform or library of content or other intellectual property.

B. EARNOUT DEFINED

In order to bridge the gap between the valuation desired by a seller and the price that the buyer is willing to pay, buyers and sellers frequently structure what is commonly called an "earnout." An earnout is essentially a contingent part of the purchase price in an M&A transaction and is only paid out if certain performance milestones are achieved. In plain terms, the buyer is essentially saying to the seller, *"You say your business is worth X and I think it is worth Y, but if the business performs over the next 1-3 years and hits various agreed milestones, I am willing to agree with you and pay X, and if not, I am only willing to pay Y."*

Typical milestones for earnouts include the achievement of EBITDA thresholds, revenue thresholds, end user thresholds, product deliveries and sometimes just plain passage of time.

C. STRUCTURING TIPS

Because earnouts have a high probability of leading to future disputes, it's important to structure them in a way that best achieves relative certainty for both parties. For sellers, it's important that they retain adequate control of the post-closing operations and are employed and empowered by the buyer in order to have the best chance at achieving their earnout milestones. If they are not employed by the buyer – or even if they are employed but don't have adequate control of the post-closing operations – sellers will have a very difficult time ensuring that the earnout is achieved.

For both parties, it is important that the earnout thresholds are objective – easily determinable by a calculation or observation that can be made by a neutral third party. Introducing any subjectivity only leads to disputes. Of course, extremes also exist. I have seen cases where the buyer's leverage is so strong that the seller's earnout is structured such that its achievement (or failure) was to be determined by the buyer's board of directors in "good faith." Without a dispute resolution mechanism in place, that kind of earnout was essentially left to the discretion of the buyer – which meant that it was potentially completely meaningless.

Earnouts form an important part of the purchase price in an M&A transaction when bridging a valuation gap is not otherwise possible, but ultimately must be structured properly to avoid dispute and capture the value intended to be achieved by both parties.

V. QUICK TIPS

Here are some "quick tips" related to a few other key deal-related topics that literally could warrant their own chapters.

A. INVESTMENTS IN LLCS

Many investments in digital media and entertainment – and even some in technology – are structured through investments in limited liability companies (or "LLCs"). While technology investments have become formulaic (either following typical convertible security or convertible note terms, or following the NVCA [National Venture Capital Association] form of investment documents), investments in LLCs are the opposite. There are no model forms or industry accepted practices for LLCs. While some general issues have become somewhat customary, overall there is no governing model set of documents.

Because of this dynamic in LLC investments, it's important for companies and investors to make sure to cover all aspects of the investment relationship in the Limited Liability Company Agreement (or Operating Agreement). This kind of agreement governs the entirety of the parties' relationship. These documents can be very simple, or they can be extraordinarily complicated – reaching in excess of 100 pages! What's important is that the parties cover a number of critical areas in order to avoid later dispute. These include: (i) management (how the company will be managed and whether there will be any minority approvals); (ii) contribution requirements; (iii) operational matters; (iv) distributions; (v) transfer restrictions (including rights of first refusal, tag-along rights, and drag-along rights ... *don't worry about those last two yet*); (vi) buy-sell arrangements in the event the parties desire to exit the relationship; and (vii) what happens in case of liquidation.

B. LIMITATIONS OF LIABILITY IN M&A

In M&A transactions, as in investment deals, the selling company (like the company seeking investment) gives representations and warranties about its business. This is the traditional way in which buyers and sellers allocate risks relating to the seller's business as it stands on the date of closing. A basic representation regarding a party's intellectual property may say, for example, that none of the seller's intellectual property ("IP") infringes the

IP of any third party. Another example of this same kind of representation may instead say that *"to the seller's knowledge,"* none of the seller's IP infringes the IP rights of others. In the first example, the seller bares all of the risk in the event that its IP actually infringes the IP of a third party on the date of closing. In the second example, the seller only bares that risk if it actually knows of any such infringement and fails to disclose it to the buyer (which failure in and of itself could be viewed as fraud in addition to a breach of a representation and warranty!).

What happens in these representations and warranties is that the seller and the buyer negotiate them until they are both happy – or both mutually unhappy – and the result ends up shifting risk to one or the other.

The way in which parties limit their overall liability for breaches of representations and warranties is by adopting a standard set of provisions that typically limit the time period after closing for parties to bring a claim for breach, and by also adopting "baskets," "mini-baskets" and "caps." I will cover those briefly here:

"Survival" – Survival provisions for representations and warranties provide that those provisions will survive for a certain exact period of time and, after that time, no claims can be made for breaches of those representations and warranties. Typical time periods for survival of most representations and warranties are 1-2 years, with the exception of certain so-called "fundamental" representations and warranties like "due authorization," "good title to assets," "capitalization" and representations relating to taxes, all of which typically survive until the expiration of the applicable statute of limitations.

"Baskets" – Baskets act as a baseline of minimum damages that a buyer must first incur before they can bring claims against the seller for breaches of representations and warranties. Baskets can be structured as a "tipping basket," which means that if a buyer experiences damages exceeding some threshold amount, it can come back and bring claims against the seller all the way back to the first dollar of damages. Baskets can also be structured as a "deductible," which acts exactly like it sounds and is commonly understood in insurance terms. This kind of deductible means that if a buyer experiences damages exceeding some threshold amount, it can only bring claims against the seller for those damages they incur in excess of that threshold amount. A tipping basket is commonly understood to be more favorable to a buyer as compared to a deductible basket.

"Mini-Baskets" – Mini-baskets are used to determine what level of damages should be counted to apply against the overall basket. For example, if a mini-basket in a transaction is $1,000, then all damages for breaches of representations and warranties that are less than $1,000 would not apply toward the basket. Mini-baskets are often used in combination with tipping baskets so as to discourage a buyer from "loading" the basket with smaller items in order to trigger its tipping point back to the first dollar of damages.

"Caps" – Caps are used to apply an overall limitation of liability for any breaches of general representations and warranties, as opposed to "fundamental" representations and warranties mentioned earlier. While buyers and sellers understand that the seller must stand behind its representations and warranties, they acknowledge that the buyer still has purchased and will benefit from the overall business and, accordingly, it is appropriate to limit the seller's liability for breaches of most representations and warranties. Typical caps for indemnification are 15% or less of the total purchase price – with the median cap size over the last several years being 10%.

From a seller's perspective, a "cap" may sometimes be understood as being a purchase price reduction. You can bet that many buyers will do whatever they can, post-closing, to uncover as many seller liabilities that they can in order to reach that cap.

Just another dose of reality for the already-complex M&A game.

Part IV

● ● ●

2017 YEAR IN REVIEW & WHERE MEDIA 2.0 IS GOING IN 2018 & BEYOND

Chapter 25

• • •

A LOOK BACK AT MY PREDICTIONS FOR 2017

Before I predict where Media 2.0 is headed in 2018, let's first reflect upon my predictions for digital media for this past year. This abbreviated scorecard gives a good snapshot of the year's key digital media developments and milestones, and also gives you an opportunity to judge for yourself how credible my prognostications are.

These were my Top 10 digital media predictions for 2017, as I laid them out last year in the first edition of this book, together with my abbreviated "listicled" summary analysis of how they stacked up to reality.

PREDICTION #1 – *We will see all-out war in the world of premium video, as both massive new entrants like AT&T's DirecTV Now – and SVOD services like Hulu – become virtual MVPDs that, like Sling TV and Sony PlayStation Vue, offer live channels to compete head-on with the actual MVPDs.*

2017 REALITY CHECK
Check. Prediction #1 realized, big time. 2017 proved to be a year of hyper-competition in the global world of premium OTT video. Hulu and YouTube were just two very different kinds of players that pushed the

button to "live" to give consumers significantly more choice to our traditional pay TV packages. Whereas we started the year with 2-3 television choices (cable, satellite and perhaps Sling TV), we ended it with more than double that (including Hulu Live, YouTube TV, and DirecTV Now). Even the traditional actual MVPDs like Comcast announced that they too will soon join the virtual MVPD fray. And, of course, Disney blew our mouse ears right off by announcing not one, but two separate SVODs forthcoming to compete head-on with Netflix. It's not just war out there. It's an all out battle royale and 2018 will bring significant casualties.

PREDICTION #2 – *Netflix's overall dominance in the world of premium OTT video will be challenged like never before, as seemingly docile competitors like Hulu beat it to this virtual MVPD expansion, as global competitors take out China and other territories before it, and as pure-play content-only monetizing business models fight to compete against an increasingly aggressive array of industry behemoths that can use content as marketing.*

2017 REALITY CHECK
Roger that. First, Hulu and YouTube launched their virtual MVPDs in 2017 (joining DirecTV Now, Sling TV, Playstation Vue and others that already offered it), while Netflix said nary a peep about any such live TV channel plans coming anytime soon. Second, these new virtual MVPDs, together with Amazon, Apple and an entirely new and seemingly never-ending host of others, now give all of us consumers real Netflix alternatives (or, at a minimum, options). And, these are spending up big time on Originals and other exclusive content to take Netflix down at least a peg or two.

Meanwhile, more multi-faceted behemoths like Disney, Comcast and Verizon announced their own upcoming premium SVOD or virtual MVPD services, with Disney even telling the world that it would no longer play nice with Netflix and license its most valuable content. Content is the new weaponry – both defensively (withholding it from others) and offensively (promoting it to differentiate from others). Apple too announced its own $1 billion dollar Originals plan. And, that's just the domestic players. The international playing field grew increasingly crowded for Netflix as well, as Chinese conglomerates like Alibaba (via its iQIYI OTT service) strengthened their claims to be the real "Netflix of China" (and Netflix had no choice but to play along), and Amazon reportedly made meaningful inroads in Europe.

PREDICTION #3 – *Mega M&A will rule the day. Consider this the "AT&T Effect," as the titans of both technology (platforms) and content (creators) react to the $85 billion acquisition of Time Warner. Netflix's long-term vulnerability means that active discussions will take place in 2017 to buy it (Disney already was rumored to be interested in 2016).*

2017 REALITY CHECK
No M&A deal this year surpassed 2016's AT&T mega $85 billion acquisition of Time Warner. But, Verizon did finally close its discounted acquisition of beleaguered Yahoo! And, Discovery Communications bought Scripps. Meanwhile, Disney chose to fight, rather than buy, Netflix. *(Hmmm, maybe that makes Apple want to buy it even more ...).*

PREDICTION #4 – *The streaming music market also consolidates further, as the "big box" multi-monetizing digital retailers (Apple, Amazon, Google/YouTube) increasingly use music as "loss leaders" and squeeze out the hopes of the remaining independents that monetize only the music itself (Spotify, Pandora, Napster, Deezer, Slacker, and a host of others).*

2017 REALITY CHECK
Behemoth digital "big-box" players' big-squeeze absolutely continued in 2017, just as predicted, as overall economics (and losses) of pure-play services Spotify

and Pandora continued their slide. SiriusXM offered a life-line to struggling and strategically-perplexed Pandora, taking a substantial piece of the company in the process. Meanwhile Spotify announced an alternative, somewhat exotic plan for going public, and yet that public event took months to materialize. Both bleed cash amidst overall unkind economics and despite streaming's now-proven ability to grow the overall music industry pie.

Artist-friendly consumer darling SoundCloud's pure-play economics, even with its massive global reach, rained down and nearly flooded the company into oblivion. The company was propped up only at the 11th hour by two financial institutions that are in the game to make tried-and-true strategic fixes to sell it off later for a significant profit. And, as year-end approached, LiveXLive signed a deal to acquire long-languishing Slacker for $50 million (a deal contingent on LiveXLive's successful public offering). All in all, hopes and dreams of the pure-play Indies dimmed further in 2017, even as they significantly fueled the overall music industry's continuing re-birth.

PREDICTION #5 – *The artificial platform distinction between short-form and long-form content will begin to disappear* (much like the "MCN" moniker disappeared in 2016), as duration no longer serves as a proxy for quality. Good storytelling is good storytelling, period.

2017 REALITY CHECK

Tough to prove this one right or wrong, but at least anecdotally, the overall industry is moving toward this mindset. Let's be clear. For most, mobile still means short-form, and lean-back living room/television means long-form. But, that's certainly not how many creators and distributors now think. That's too black and white. Rather, what stories can work on what individual platform without overt constraints of space and time? That's the right way to think about it. And, increasingly Media 2.0'ers in our multi-platform world do. The best of them think of it all holistically – developing stories that can seamlessly travel across all platforms (and then back again) in a content-fueled virtuous cycle.

PREDICTION #6 – *The artificial distinction between media compa-nies, and the advertisers who support them, also blurs.* *Every brand can be a media company, because ultimately each brand tells stories. And, they increasingly work with digital-first media companies that increasingly target them to get there.*

2017 REALITY CHECK

No question about this reality either. Digital advertising spending in the U.S. surpassed television ad spending for the first time in 2016 ($72.5 bil-lion compared to $71.3 billion), and brands increasingly bypass the major traditional agencies to engage directly with consumers. To punctuate this point, in August 2017, shares of global ad agency juggernaut WPP experi-enced their biggest drop in 17 years.

Virtually all major consumer brands now develop "branded content" – product-laden content that speaks authentically, is not force-fed, and is compelling (entertaining, educational) in its own right and, therefore, highly social and share-worthy. Essentially, content as commerce. The trick is to create brand love and loyalty, of course. And, brands increas-ingly follow the lead of digital-first studios – working with them and learn-ing from them to turn that trick into commercial reality. Several brands increasingly do it themselves. Continuous Media 2.0 engagement, experi-mentation, and data-mining may get them to the promised land even more efficiently, and more powerfully.

PREDICTION #7 – *VR & AR, both of which brashly and loud-ly broke out into the early commercial mainstream in 2016, will* *maintain a slightly lower profile in 2017. Yet, the technology will evolve significantly, and the live content that brings that technology to life will begin to reveal itself in tantalizing new ways. And, both media companies and VCs will increasingly pour money into the content development side of the VR and AR space.*

2017 REALITY CHECK

Prediction becomes reality, yet again. VR headsets untethered themselves in significant numbers in 2017, while AR's first-wave of innovation – the software platform layer – quietly invaded our smart phone hardware in overwhelming numbers thanks to our favorite three omnipresent behemoth amigos – Apple, Google and Facebook. Studios also accelerated their investments in new immersive content-focused think-tanks and studios (like FoxNet), and investors continued to throw boatloads of real cold hard cash to a burgeoning number of promising live action VR startups experimenting with spherical storytelling. Meanwhile, across the Pacific, China's BAT goliaths (Baidu, Alibaba and Tencent) commit massively themselves to the promise of immersive. So, while perhaps 2017 reflected less VR and AR "style" (we had no single *Pokemon Go*-like global mega-moment-in-time), this year certainly featured much more "substance."

PREDICTION #8 – *eSports' relentless march forward will accelerate too*, *as brands will divert significantly more resources to this new "space" which, in turn, will increasingly challenge the traditional sports market.*

2017 REALITY CHECK

No doubt about this one either. More media companies and strategic investors – as well as plain old gamblers – made big bets on eSports and its longevity. And, more e-thletes scored big, both in terms of wins and in cash. The overall industry was expected to balloon to nearly $700 million by year-end 2017 (up 41.3%), just like the size of The Grinch's little heart multiplied on Christmas Day.

PREDICTION #9 – *The power of data becomes increasingly clear and critical to Media 2.0 companies, and consolidation here too will rule the day. Players across the Media 2.0 ecosystem (content creators, distributors, marketers) will benefit from that disruption via more choice and less cost to gain a deeper understanding of (and develop greater personalization for) specifically targeted consumers.*

2017 REALITY CHECK

While I can't point to any specific mega-M&A event that supported this one in 2017, suffice it to say that Media 2.0 companies across the overall ecosystem became increasingly data-driven in 2017 (as they should). Certainly, all eyes (both Media 1.0 and Media 2.0) are now on Netflix, Amazon, Facebook and others that have demonstrated massive commercial and artistic success by using their ever-more massive treasure troves of data about everything we do to actively guide their overall content development and media strategies. Hollywood's most prestigious awards increasingly find their way into the hands of those former nerds (and I mean that as a compliment).

PREDICTION #10 – *International becomes an even greater battleground, as the largest Media 2.0 players both inside and outside the U.S. increasingly encroach on each other's home turf. As a result, companies big and small will be more willing to partner with players outside their borders to compete most effectively against these forces and to significantly expand their own opportunities.*

2017 REALITY CHECK

Amen to this one. Netflix partnered with Chinese OTT video leader iQ-IYI to establish at least some sort of meaningful presence in that invaluable territory. Some of Japan's leading and competing media companies banded together to beat back Netflix on their turf. And, a multi-national cast of characters did the same with iflix to arrive ahead of Netflix in untapped and under-appreciated emerging markets.

All in all, mission accomplished in terms of my 2017 predictions *(as self-serving as I know that sounds)*.

Now, onto 2017's most **fearless** Media 2.0 companies that drove these overall trends, innovations, and realities. The ones that boldly went where too few were willing to go … at least so far.

Chapter 26

● ● ●

2017'S "FEARLESS FIVE"

If nothing else, my goal with this book is to emphasize Media 2.0's possibilities – and the urgency to take bold action to seize transformational opportunities and reach new heights of creativity, impact, and overall "success" *(however YOU define it)*.

With that in mind, welcome to my second edition of the **"Fearless Five"** – the five companies in the Media 2.0 world that I believe made the boldest and most audacious moves of the year. That doesn't mean that these companies ultimately will be the most successful. But, it does mean that they were the most fearless and placed the biggest Media 2.0 bets in 2017. I name them in order of "audacity."

#1 MOST FEARLESS – AMAZON – This behemoth didn't even make it onto my **Fearless Five** list last year (although I did give it "honorable mention" status together with Comcast NBCUniversal, which didn't make either cut this year). But, Amazon's Media 2.0 audacity was unrivaled in 2017. In fact, Amazon is the single most "under the radar" mega-force in the Media 2.0 world. Amazon now absolutely places content (premium video, UGC video, live streaming, and streaming music) front and center in its quest to open up its virtual mega-mall to all of us (and keep us there). It now rivals even mighty Netflix in terms of its willingness to spend on Originals and global expansion to inject meaningful fear into the market leader.

And, Amazon's treasure trove of data about each of us – like Facebook's – is detailed and directly tied to our identities. In Amazon's case, it is tied to every single detail of every single product search and purchase – an invaluable rich record of our shopping habits, reflecting how willing we are to part with our cash (and for what). Don't forget Amazon's massively successful Echo and Alexa's now-ubiquitous voice, not to mention the staying power of its Kindle. And, oh yes, in 2017 we watched its awe-inspiring multi-platform moves in the offline physical world with its release of Originals in our movie theaters, its construction of brick and mortar Amazon Stores in our shopping malls, and its somewhat mind-boggling acquisition of Whole Foods. All I can say is, *"Yowza!"*

#2 MOST FEARLESS – FACEBOOK – Facebook jumped two spots from #4 last year, because this Media 2.0 Goliath continued to make massive bets to transform itself into being a full-fledged major media force. After experimenting with video big-time in 2016, Facebook launched its new television-like Watch service in 2017 to its gazillions of constantly-engaged users (which means virtually all of us) with a significant investment of premium television-like dollars on its own Originals to seed the new service.

Traditional media and advertising companies took note, realizing the giant's virtually un-matchable knowledge of the minute details of each of our lives, including our hopes and dreams. That's dream targeting of content and ads, man. Speaking of ads, Facebook, together with Google, now owns nearly 2/3 of the global digital advertising market. And, I haven't even mentioned Facebook's increasingly aggressive forays into its next great frontier – VR and AR. Immersive is Facebook's "next big thing," as it tries to co-opt that VR/AR opportunity from Apple and continue its evolution from text – to still images – to video – to 360 degree video – and continuing into immersive.

#3 MOST FEARLESS – ALIBABA – No international Media 2.0 giants made my list last year, but not because they didn't deserve to. Rather, merely because last year's inaugural version of this book almost exclusively focused on U.S.-based companies. I corrected course significantly this year (although still not enough), and when I look across our borders, I see Alibaba as representing the same kind of full force, power and fearlessness that define Fearless #1 and Fearless #2 above. Alibaba, like Facebook, is a social media giant amongst giants in its territory (China) that towers over the U.S. in terms of sheer potential reach.

And, like Facebook, Alibaba drove even more success in 2017 in its quest to be a massive premium OTT video force, securing its Netflix partnership and investing massively in its own Originals. Alibaba also commit to billions and billions of dollars more for VR and AR both for content/experience development, but also for e-commerce. After all, Alibaba's bread and butter – its ultimate raison d'etre *(I don't know how to say that in Mandarin, so I'll at least use another international language to connote a non-U.S. bias)* – is the same as Amazon's. Invite the masses to buy everything – and I mean, everything – from one source.

#4 MOST FEARLESS – NETFLIX – This premium OTT video leader dropped one spot from #3 to #4 this year, which may not sound like much – but which is absolutely intended to signify a real strategic shift for its overall place in the Media 2.0 world as 2017 ends. If nothing else, this book justifies some very real paranoia in the ranks of Netflix's management and investors, because virtually all other global behemoths are absolutely out to get them. And, as we have seen, many of them carry weapons and boast resources that Netflix can't match. Certainly not on its own.

Nevertheless, Netflix fearlessly marches onward to prove me and other doubters wrong *(I respect that)*. First, it is expanding 2017's already eye-popping $6 billion commitment to Originals to $7-$8 billion in 2018 (and with $17 billion in overall content commitments already locked and loaded). Second, CEO Reed Hastings stoically tells investors that Netflix will continue to burn boatloads of cash for years and years to come in pursuit of those ends and to beat back the proliferating global competition. That's the very definition of "fearless."

#5 MOST FEARLESS – OTTER MEDIA/AT&T – Okay, this one is a bit of a "cheat," because these two are separate, yet related, companies *(at least as I write this, since rumors also swirled in 2017 that AT&T was looking to acquire Otter)*. Remember, Otter Media is the 50/50 Media 2.0 joint venture of The Chernin Group and AT&T. AT&T, last year's **Fearless Five** champion, dropped 4 spots to #5 this year. After all, anyone would find it difficult to follow-up last year's 1-2 Media 2.0 punch to the guts of all others – its $85 billion acquisition of Time Warner and its launch of virtual MVPD DirecTV Now with pricing that rocked the worlds of all others entering the space.

Nonetheless, AT&T continued to fearlessly build its case this year, and certainly remains a dominating force that touches us in myriad ways (mobile/wireless, wired, pay TV, premium OTTs, and content creator/media company). It will extend its reach significantly further into our lives with Hulu (OTT), Jaunt (VR) and Magic Leap (AR) when its Time Warner mega-deal closes. So, AT&T continues to be everywhere it wants to be.

Meanwhile, Otter Media continues to intrigue me with its own premium OTT video services (Fullscreen, Crunchyroll), digital-first studios (Rooster Teeth, Gunpowder & Sky), and the picks and shovels technology that supports them. Let's not forget that Otter wraps them all up with an intriguing foundational philosophy ("brand love") and truly multi-platform strategy (monetization not only via online advertising, subscriptions and branded content, but also via real-world physical merchandising and live events).

So, there it is. Like last year, many "honorable mentions" almost made the cut, most notably Apple and Disney for all the reasons I discuss earlier in this book – including Apple's potential AR domination, and Disney's direct pursuit of its SVOD ambitions. Meanwhile, AR's enigmatic Magic Leap, last year's #2, fell completely off my list this year, simply because it continued down its enigmatic path to a destination still unknown (and, therefore, was simply too difficult to evaluate against the others). No doubt many of you may think that one or more on my list aren't worthy – while others definitely are – but, hey, it's my book – and these are *my* **Fearless Five** companies that I applaud most for pure cojones.

Let me know what you think. Which ones I missed. Which ones I didn't. And, which ones on my list aren't deserving. Send your thoughts to me at peter@creatv.media. I want to hear from you.

Who will make the cut next year? More international players? Less obvious players? Perhaps even some startups?

Will be fun to watch – and perhaps even actively influence in 2018.

Chapter 27

● ● ●

MY TOP 10 MEDIA 2.0 PREDICTIONS FOR 2018

Now onto my Top 10 Media 2.0 Predictions for 2018 – my 5th Annual prognostications *(the first three appeared in media and tech publications)*. This is where I put myself out there, after synthesizing the various strands of what I have seen and heard throughout the year – including from top executives, entrepreneurs, creators, and influencers in the Media 2.0 world.

Drumroll please!

PREDICTION #1 – There will be blood in the escalating battle amongst premium OTT video giants, as the market becomes over-saturated, early winners and losers are declared, and Netflix finds itself increasingly in everyone's lines of sight – including Disney's and Apple's.

Originals continue to be the primary weapon used on the OTT video battlefront, extending Media 2.0's "New Golden Age" for creators and further skyrocketing content-related development and production costs (including the price tags for A-list marquee talent). Content also increasingly begins to be used defensively, like Disney withholding its crown jewels from Netflix. Meanwhile, the newly expanded list of virtual MVPDs will fix their initial flaws and offer consumers real competitive choice. Whereas we started 2016 with 2-3 real, viable mainstream choices in the U.S. for live TV – and 2017 with 6-7 viable choices for our television viewing (cable, satellite, Hulu Live, YouTube TV, DirecTV Now, Sling TV) – we will end 2018 with 10 or more for each of us.

We already know that the traditional actual MVPDs, like Comcast, will enter the fray in 2018, as will Disney when it launches its own pair of "Netflix Killers." But, Apple almost certainly will also join the premium SVOD fray in 2018. Apple cannot live on Apple TV alone. It feels it must own its own premium SVOD and will either launch its own "Apple Video" service or simply buy Netflix or Hulu. And I haven't even mentioned any of the massive international players yet, but don't overlook those. They include Baidu's iQIYI which is mulling over a U.S.-based IPO for 2018.

It's all-out war in the premium OTT video world, as cord-cutting accelerates and traditional cable and satellite providers shed more paying subs. But, those traditionalists will increasingly take solace in the fact that consumers endlessly crave faster and faster broadband that will continue to lift their overall revenues and profits. Counter-intuitive, perhaps, but a very real positive consequence of Media 2.0 for them.

PREDICTION #2A – "Brand love" increasingly becomes the goal of several premium OTT video players that hope to carve out their own winning formula that differentiates, entrances, and monetizes at scale amidst the OTT clutter and noise.

Several leading OTT video services – including so-called "niche" or segment focused players – will smartly attempt to achieve real emotional connections with their consumers. These "activists" will try to convert them into becoming passionate fans who are invested in the service's identity and overall success amongst giants, and who can be monetized in true multi-platform fashion. That means not only via ads and subscriptions, but also live events and merchandising *(a form of participatory content)*. You can bet that Disney – the single most multi-platform of all Media 2.0 companies *(although Amazon is catching up fast, as we have seen)* – will place its global brand front and center in its upcoming SVOD war. Finally, product personalization also becomes an area of increasing focus, so that my user experience is different from yours on the same platform (rather than the traditional one-size-fits-all broadcasting-style form of viewer engagement).

BONUS PREDICTION #2B – Most other new premium OTT video market entrants in this beyond-crowded premium OTT video space will be swallowed up or simply languish, squeezed out by market leaders and the sheer scale of Google and Facebook, with which they simply can't compete for ad dollars.

Many of the so-called niche-focused OTT services still primarily rely upon ad dollars, but remember, Google and Facebook already own about 2/3 of that global digital advertising market. That means that most OTT video players simply cannot succeed on ad dollars alone – and other means of monetization will be beyond their reach because they fail to deliver a sufficiently compelling, differentiated and emotionally connected media experience. Winners will swallow up losers in an environment of accelerating M&A *(see Prediction #5 below)*.

PREDICTION #3 – The Hollywood community (motion pictures and television) will begin to increasingly understand the power of new cost-effective Media 2.0-related ways to test and measure new characters, stories and engagement first on a smaller scale, in order to more smartly and efficiently place their big expensive bets.

Innovative new services like comics-driven motion book company "Madefire," mobile-first horror-focused company "Crypt TV," and mobile-focused text storytelling company "Yarn" – all discussed earlier in this book – point the way. Meanwhile, Netflix, Amazon and Facebook will continue to mine their deep data about all of our hopes and dreams to maximize "hits" and minimize "misses" as compared to traditionalists. And, they will increasingly do a good job at it, as they become more confident in their creative pursuits.

PREDICTION #4 – Spotify will go public at a lofty valuation, but those numbers and overall investor confidence will decline throughout the course of the year, together with Pandora's, as these two pure-play global streaming music leaders find it increasingly difficult to compete against "big box" behemoths Apple, Amazon and Google/YouTube.

Yes, Spotify and Pandora boast massive scale. Yet, scale alone does not financial success make. In fact, pure-play distribution success leads to higher and higher losses due to sobering industry economics these pure-plays can't stomach, but the behemoths can due to their multi-pronged business models. These harsh realities mean that investors of many pure-play streaming services will take a hard look at themselves in 2018 as they contemplate their strategic next steps. Many will realize that they can't go it alone. And that leads to M&A, which brings me to …

PREDICTION #5 – One company's struggles are another company's opportunity, and successful "bigger fish" will step up their M&A efforts to acquire those Media 2.0 companies that see no long-term path to making it on their own.

M&A is a hallmark of Media 2.0's overall digital, multi-platform tech-infused transformation of the media and entertainment business. Just like AT&T acquired storied traditional (yet slow-moving) Time Warner in 2016 and Verizon acquired ubiquitous (yet stumbling) Yahoo! in 2017, expect some more massive deals in 2018, together with a number of smaller, but significant, deals. And don't just look within U.S. borders. There is no virtual wall in our borderless Media 2.0 world, which means that the pace of M&A will accelerate internationally as well. To be clear, not all M&A will flow from weakness. Sometimes the numbers offered simply will be too high to reject. But make no mistake. Weakness will abound amidst hyper-competition.

PREDICTION #6 – Data finally becomes a high profile, high priority "missing link" in the strategies of most Media 2.0 players who, accordingly, will try to correct course.

Virtually all traditional media and entertainment companies now openly covet Netflix's, Amazon's and Facebook's user data, as well as how those services leverage that data to their seemingly-untouchable advantage. The quest for data – and the services that provide, analyze and inform – takes on new urgency amongst the traditional media and entertainment ranks. Prediction #3 above offers some tantalizing clues regarding new ways to leverage data to create characters and content that resonate more effectively (and cost-effectively).

PREDICTION #7 – Brave new technologies like AI and machine learning (via virtual assistants Alexa, Siri and Google) enter the mainstream and increasingly impact the Media 2.0 worlds of media, entertainment and advertising, while blockchain technology captures industry mind-share and begins to infiltrate mainstream Media 2.0 conversations.

The soothing voices of Alexa and Siri *(sorry Google, yours is a little less so)* guide us through this AI/machine learning revolution. "Virtual assistants," "smart speakers" (or whatever you want to call them) will increasingly populate our homes – improve significantly over time – and serve up our favorite content (as well as increasingly targeted and hoped-to-be "welcomed" incentives, promotions and ads).

More exotically, AI already develops movie trailers that some believe approach the impact of their human-generated counterparts. You be the judge – check out the first AI-produced movie trailer, care of IBM's Watson, for the fittingly AI-themed 2016 motion picture thriller *Morgan* (and just imagine how much AI has advanced since then).

So, AI may become a real threat to even creative pursuits that, up to this point, have been considered to be untouchable by computers, bots, and robots. In fact, if Elon Musk is right – and at the risk of sounding a bit dystopian *(forgive me, I just read more tweets from a certain house in D.C.)* – AI may be an ultimate global threat to us all. Musk tweeted in 2017 that *"Competition for AI superiority at national level most likely cause of WW3 imo"* (note – that is Musk's Twitter-speak, not errors in my transcription of it). Yikes for Hollyworld – and Yikes for the World itself ….

Sounding a happier note (although certainly not happy for all), the voice of blockchain technology – barely acknowledged in Media 2.0 circles in 2017 – will increasingly be heard and respected at the water cooler. Blockchain technology conceptually holds revolutionary and industry-transforming new offensive and defensive power. On the offensive front, blockchain will enable completely new ways to monetize content via cryptocurrency and direct creator-to-consumer distribution (*sans* today's leading middlemen). And, on the defensive front, blockchain promises to eradicate piracy.

PREDICTION #8 – Behemoths Apple, Google and Facebook will increase their already-massive investments in immersive technologies, and 2018 will be AR's break-out year in terms of forced mass adoption

via ARKit, ARCore and Camera Effects Platform which give our mobile phones real "spatial sense" as true AR systems.

VCs and strategic investors will also continue to throw boatloads of cash into the overall immersive space, hoping to fuel the development of real world live entertainment and storytelling, and not only games. And, AR's gold rush also means continued growth in the related "wearables" market and early, very early, consumer adoption of AR-driven eyewear. The immersive market opportunity is still so nascent, yet its ultimate promise is so great, that the money trying to capture it in 2018 will be seemingly endless. And, when a market together invests so heavily, a market becomes our consumer reality.

PREDICTION #9 – Good old basic, rudimentary text-based services and audio podcasts will continue to astound in terms of both scale and counter-programming success.

These forms of media face no significant licensing or royalty headwinds, unlike video and music streaming services. That means that all money that flows from them, flows directly into the pockets of service providers. And, the most successful of these services can scale massively, meaning that monetization can be significant. Very. That's why text-centric storytelling apps like Wattpad are on fire right now, and why Spotify launched a song-texting feature in 2017. Spotify also introduced a new podcast element to its overall growth story (as did Pandora, by the way). Such attempts to diversify are the only hope for pure-plays, at least as independent stand-alone entities.

PREDICTION #10 – The too often-overlooked, yet potentially game-changing, live event and venue plank of truly holistic and 360-degree multi-platform strategies increasingly becomes noticed and offline experiments build.

Call this the "Amazon Effect," as players across the Media 2.0 ecosystem stop scratching their heads about, and rather begin studying, Amazon's direct-to-theater motion picture releases, brick and mortar retail stores, and Whole Foods super-stores. Amazon understands what most still haven't even considered – that direct, non-virtual offline consumer engagement may be the most impactful plank of them all – bringing online engagement into the real world – and then back again to create a virtual cycle of brand engagement and consumer monetization every step of the way. Otter Media's Ellation brand has made this live event plank a cornerstone for each of its respective companies for these reasons.

In reaction to significant negative forces that permeated much of 2017, many companies will begin to take things even further by infusing their offline efforts with social impact, an inspirational and motivational element that is already proven to be commercially smart. Such fully-realized efforts hold the tantalizing power to transform Media 2.0's virtual cycle into a fully-realized multi-platform virtuous circle. Double bottom line – profitable both commercially, and societally.

Hey, Media 2.0 companies. Don't underestimate the power of humanizing your efforts with a healthy dose of offline "soul."

SUMMARY

So, 2018 certainly will push 2017's boundaries noticeably further – although these changes will be barely noticeable compared to the seismic shifts to follow in the next ten years leading up to 2028. I close with Paramount Futurist Ted Schilowitz's perspective on all of this. Ted points to two phenomena, what he calls: (1) *"the known unknown"* and (2) *"the ten year curve."* Concept 1 refers to what he calls the *"scary"* fact that we all know that massive tech-driven change is coming, but we don't know the *"twists and turns that get us there."* Meanwhile, Concept 2 refers to *"big dynamic change waves"* that he contends follow ten-year cycles. In Ted's view, we just finished the YouTube and iPhone 10-year cycles where essentially everyone around the globe now participates in those phenomena.

Ted predicts the next 10-year cycle to include "wearables" as one primary sea-change in our everyday technology-fueled interaction with content. Think AR eyewear – in all of its coming forms – in that regard. With less sophistication, I simply predict that AI and machine learning will begin to completely freak us out in the next decade.

What will be the twists and turns that get us there?

Pick up next year's *Media 2.0 (19)* to find out ….

Part V

● ● ●

SO, WHAT DO I DO NOW?

Chapter 28

● ● ●

HOW TO ACT FEARLESSLY IN 2018 AND BEYOND

At the beginning of this book – which ultimately is a journey through the disruptive, but ultimately empowering and transformational new world of Media 2.0 – I defined my main goal being to give you a firm foundation and framework to understand those forces around you. And then to motivate you, your teams, your companies to act on those forces to fully and fearlessly leverage Media 2.0's power and potential. Perhaps even give you some concrete ideas, concepts, strategies and examples to help get you there.

Now that you've reached these final pages *(whew!)*, hopefully you fully embrace this call to arms and are ready to take action. Boldly. But, you also may be asking, "*how?*" and "*where do I begin?*"

First, I urge you to carefully re-read specific sections of this book – like Part III's "News You Can Use" – that lay out concrete concepts and examples for you to consider. I identify many that are immediately actionable. I also urge you to deeply study the actions of others – especially market leaders and losers *(sound too Trump-ian?)* – to uncover meaningful, impactful clues of where the Media 2.0 world is going. The predictions and realities I lay out in Chapters 25 and 27 may be particularly helpful here.

But, perhaps most fundamentally, prioritize your Media 2.0 efforts right now. Clearly and loudly communicate that mandate to all key stakeholders. Build – and then empower – the best possible teams to think outside of the box and aggressively drive those efforts forward. As part of these new "innovation" teams, you understandably may want to (and likely should) work closely with focused and experienced outside, objective experts and advisors – advisors who can: deliver critical proprietary market intelligence; help educate and motivate your teams and transform company culture; strategize and organize priorities; optimize and execute actions; connect and make key introductions to decision-makers, innovators and influencers; and maximize new opportunities, revenue growth, and overall operational success and market leadership.

Ultimately, it all comes down to people. So, job one is to identify and hire the best. And then invest in them. Don't be cheap. Don't think you're saving money by not getting the best. You aren't. You're leaving significant money (and potentially game-changing opportunities) on the table with each passing day they aren't on your side. Even worse, you may be putting your company further at risk by falling further behind. With the right team, your active investment will be rewarded with significant, and potentially transformational, change and demonstrable ROI *(remember to measure everything, right?)*.

Finally, heed Media 2.0's fundamental lesson and universal truth. Those who act now, will win. Those who don't, won't. So, chart your path. And, no matter whichever path you choose, make sure you "just do it." Boldly.

IT'S TIME TO BE FEARLESS!

Epilogue

• • •

A PERSONAL NOTE FOR OUR INCREASINGLY DIGITAL, VIRTUAL AGE

My wife Luisa and I have watched the John Cusack movie *"High Fidelity"* several times. Classic movie for any music lover for many reasons – not the least of which is that it unleashed hilarious Jack Black into the world. In the film, Cusack plays the owner of a vintage record shop who is part slacker, part hopeless romantic, and part simply confused by life – but a 100 percent believer in the power of music and compelling content in general *(something I wholeheartedly share)*.

Cusack recounts the "Top 10" romantic breakups of his life, and essentially sets each one to music. He is an avid creator of mix tapes *(remember those?)* and agonizes over every single individual track he adds to create the most impactful and meaningful "whole." He literally caresses the vinyl and plucks out tracks he deems worthy to establish the perfect overall vibe of what he experienced in that particular moment in his life, and with that particular romantic entanglement.

And, that got me thinking about that old mix tape. I vividly recall those days when I too spent hours with my vinyl creating that perfect mix tape that was meaningful to me and hopefully someone else. So much effort was put into this process. So much thought. So much nurturing. You see, it wasn't easy to make them. You needed to manually select the right album, pull out the vinyl, select the right tracks, and place the needle down onto the vinyl on the perfect spot, meld track to track, fade them in and out to the next one, write the name of each track on the cassette's sleeve, and, then, ultimately *(and the crescendo to the entire process)* come up with the perfect title for that mix tape.

That perfect title was particularly critical if your mix tape was intended to be given to someone else, because the goal was to make an impact. This all was time-consuming both physically – and frequently emotionally. You sweat the details. Why? Because each individual mix tape mattered. You couldn't simply churn them out one after another. Volumes were low, as in number of personalized tapes – not in the sound itself, which you frequently cranked to a Spinal Tap-ian 11. But, the "love for the game" was high.

And, here's the thing. The person to whom you gave your beloved mix tape – be it a friend, or your girlfriend or boyfriend at the time – knew it. They knew how hard you worked to make that tape. They inherently understood all of the steps involved. All that care and feeding. And that's why it made such a deep impact on them. It was meaningful. And, that was the point.

Fast forward to today and to the Media 2.0 world that I love – and in which I have deeply immersed myself both professionally and personally *(hence, this book, which itself comes in two flavors – eBook for sure, but good old-fashioned print as well so that you can actually feel the pages and my mom can place it on her actual bookshelf)*. Yes, digital gives us so much power. Yes, digital gives us so much access. So much discovery. So much control.

But, sometimes too much?

Think about today's digital music playlists that we share. Yes, of course, we frequently give them some thought. Perhaps many of you give some of them much thought. But, the amount of effort, the amount of expenditure of time, and the amount of care and feeding are entirely different. Digital is comparatively easy. We can simply find and select individual tracks in rapid fire and churn out playlist after playlist, and then share them not only individually, but also with the entire world with one swipe of our smart phone.

It is precisely that mass volume. That mass sharing. And, that physical ease and fractional time commitment that make each playlist less impactful. Less impactful to you as the playlist creator, and less impactful to any one person with whom you share it.

This "lost art of the playlist" serves as an allegory of life in a sense. Digital is incredibly powerful. Sharing your musical tastes with the world is cool, very cool, indeed. But, something also is left behind unless there is pause, reflection, and dedication to seeking out some kind of "soul" to augment that power. To disconnect. Get away from the virtual. To get into the "real" and feel – literally, *feel*, something tangible.

That's why vinyl is making a comeback. That's why Amoeba Records in Los Angeles and other remaining labor of love "mom and pop" record stores have staged a small, but growing, revival. According to last year's RIAA mid-year report, vinyl sales continued their upward trajectory in 2017, now comprising 29% of total physical retail sales – their highest share since the mid-1980's when CDs began to take over. Something special and impactful happens when you actually dive into those stacks of vinyl records and sift through them. Time almost stands still. Hours go by. I've seen it with my own teen kids. They feel at home with that vinyl. At peace *(as metaphysical as that sounds)*. Just this past August 2017, my college-bound daughter Hunter actively sought out Amoeba Records in Berkeley as we toured the campus. And, we all happily obliged.

To be clear, this is not an indictment of digital. Not at all. Digital's power is real. Digital's opportunities are massive. I respect it. Generally love it *(in fact, I am streaming music as I write this)*.

But, for me, and for my "experiences," digital is frequently just the beginning. The introduction. My experiences need to be augmented with more. With effort. With dedication. With "soul." Taken outside into the physical world. With real *non*-virtual human connection and interaction. It takes a lot of work and commitment to prepare for, attend, and endure a music festival. But, boy is it worth it! My family and I will never forget our day-long journey literally across Iceland's frozen tundra to experience a DJ spinning deep down inside a glacier as part of 2016' "Secret Solstice" festival. Those kinds of experiences last a life-time. And my family is so much closer because of them.

And, for me, that's what "It" is all ultimately about.

Vinyl – and the mix tape – represent that same kind of dedication. That's why you gotta watch *(re-watch?) High Fidelity*. Be inspired by it. Finding it certainly won't be difficult in our Media 2.0 world, that's for sure. You can stream it on demand right now from any one of your favorite OTT services and on any one of your multiple devices.

"And one more thing!" *(I say, in an obvious Media 2.0 homage to Mr. Jobs).* Go outside and watch the sunset tonight.

The real thing far surpasses the digital version that your friend just posted on Facebook last night.

Made in the USA
Middletown, DE
22 November 2017